THE LOVE DRIVEN MAN

How to open your heart to what matters eternally

by

Marek Rudak
www.cs1mindset.com

THE LOVE DRIVEN MAN

Copyright ©2020 Marek Rudak

All Rights Reserved

Created by Marek Rudak

Printed by Kindle Direct Publishing 2020

First Edition 2020

No part of this document may be reproduced or transmitted in any form or by any means, electronic or mechanical, for any purpose, except by written permission of the author.

Cover design by Kirk Johnson.

Edited by Rich Marsh of Tidewater Productions. LLC.

All the drawings in Chapter 4 of this book are licensed from Sohelchy2008. All rights reserved. Sohelchy2008 is a commercial artist at https://www.fiverr.com

The author created the diagram in Chapter 7.

Scripture Citations:

Scripture quotations marked (**BSB**) are from The Holy Bible, Berean Study Bible, BSB Copyright ©2016, 2018 by Bible Hub Used by Permission. All Rights Reserved Worldwide.

Scripture quotations marked (**ESV**) are from The ESV® Bible (The Holy Bible, English Standard Version®), copyright © 2001 by Crossway, a publishing ministry of Good News Publishers. Used by permission. All rights reserved.

Scripture quotations marked (**NASB**) are taken from the NEW AMERICAN STANDARD BIBLE(R), Copyright © 1960,1962,1963,1968,1971,1972,1973,1975,1977,1995 by The Lockman Foundation. Used by permission. All rights reserved,

Scripture quotations marked (**NIV**) are taken from the Holy Bible, New International Version®, NIV®. Copyright © 1973, 1978, 1984, 2011 by Biblica, Inc.™ Used by permission of Zondervan. All rights reserved worldwide. www.zondervan.com The "NIV" and "New International Version" are trademarks registered in the United States Patent and Trademark Office by Biblica, Inc.™

Scripture quotations marked (**NLT**) are taken from the Holy Bible, New Living Translation, copyright © 1996, 2004, 2007, 2013, 2015 by Tyndale House Foundation. Used by permission of Tyndale House Publishers, Inc., Carol Stream, Illinois 60188. All rights reserved.

Scripture quotations marked (**NRSV**) are from the New Revised Standard Version Bible, copyright © 1989 National Council of the Churches of Christ in the United States of America. Used by permission. All rights reserved worldwide. http://nrsvbibles.org/

Scripture quotations marked (**NRSVCE**) are from the New Revised Standard Version Bible: Catholic Edition, copyright © 1989, 1993 National Council of the Churches of Christ in the United States of America. Used by permission. All rights reserved worldwide.

To my parents who gave me life and set me up for success

and

To my wife who inspires me when I'm weak

MAREK RUDAK

Table of Contents

Introduction: The Two Choice Routes 1
Chapter 1: Your Godly Identity 8
Chapter 2: Growing Closer to God 21
Chapter 3: Partnering with Women 36
Chapter 4: Transforming the Pain 48
Chapter 5: Taking Steps of Faith 64
Chapter 6: Keeping God #1 78
Chapter 7: Taking Action 90
Chapter 8: Progress Measurement 102
Parting Words 112
Appendix A: Additional Resources 115
Appendix B: The Love Driven Man Reflection Summary 116
   Chapter 1: Your Godly Identity 117
   Chapter 2: Growing Closer to God 118
   Chapter 3: Partnering with Women 119
   Chapter 4: Transforming the Pain 120
   Chapter 5: Taking Steps of Faith 121
   Chapter 6: Keeping God #1 122
   Chapter 7: Taking Action 123
   Chapter 8: Progress Measurement 124
About the Author 125
End Notes 126

Introduction: The Two Choice Routes

The Control Driven Man
Vs. The Love Driven Man

"Some trust in chariots, and some in horses, but we trust in the name of the Lord our God."
Psalm 20:7 (NIV)

God designed men for greatness.

You knew that before now. Go back to when you were younger.

What was your answer to the question, *"Who do you want to be when you grow up?"*

I'm sure whatever it was, it was filled with adventure, mastery, and a great sense of fulfillment.

I'm probably a lot like you. When I was younger, I wanted to be a hero. Just like the heroes in the popular 1980's action films, I wanted to be the one who saved the day. I was a bit vague on whether I would be a military commando, a karate master, or Batman. That would likely depend on which movie I had seen most recently. What would always be consistent though, was the image of myself overcoming insurmountable odds and then humbly riding off into the sunset, until the next adventure.

I was able to live out at least some of that dream. I went to West Point, graduated from Ranger School, and deployed to two combat zones. My experiences were far from the movie set glamour, but I did my part to the best of my abilities. I found, however, that the older I got, the more difficult it became for me to make my dreams a reality.

As my age number grew, so did my preference for controlling risk. I began to think that "adult" heroes invest in tangible assets, like a house, a 401(k), and a predictable career. These are today's equivalents of the chariots and horses from Psalm 20:7 that I quoted above. Adventure is fun, but as I got older, I felt increased pressure to show something for my efforts. Grown-up heroes should be able to show the fruits of their labor. If I have no concrete fruits, then was I that much of a hero?

What happened? Did I just become greedy? That's a way to look at it. Probably a more objective assessment is to say that as I got older, I started to lose belief in my potential. I felt like I had peaked, so I began to tightly control what I had. I focused on avoiding mistakes. As a kid, who cares if you're way off when acting out action movies? It just feels awesome. Even our ordered society allows kids to play.

As an adult, however, the societal expectations tighten. Now we have commitments. How is shadow boxing going to help us pay the bills, get a degree, or grow our professional network? In the adult world of competing priorities, the highest return on investment activity will typically win. Something we were all oblivious to as kids.

As a child, I listened to my heart. I lived out something that God has wired into each of us at birth - an innate desire to find and pursue our unique mission in this world. At an early age I began watching action movies, playing video games, and learning about computers. It was nothing unusual, no big deal, I just felt naturally drawn to these activities. To me they were a *"call to adventure."* But then my heart became infected with a *"disease"* I call *"fear of failure."* I caught it from an abusive grandfather who always found something wrong in me. Instead of teaching me how to use my mind to develop what was natural to my heart, my grandfather scared me into conforming to his impossible expectations. I began to use my mind to find ways to fit in. As a child, I learned that when I don't conform to what other people expect of me, I get criticized. Criticism causes pain, so controlling other people's perceptions of me is the best way to keep others away from my wounded heart, myself included.

So, I focused on building an accomplishment wall around my heart. While I am very proud to have served in the Army, I realize now that my real reason for joining the Army was to prove to others that I was strong enough. I figured that military training would make me criticism-proof. Nobody would question my manhood if I got enough badges and tabs on my uniform. This continued in corporate America. If I earned enough money, no one would criticize me. That's why I picked jobs for the paycheck, not for what God had wired into my heart. I laughed at people who followed their dreams. I thought they were simply irresponsible. Responsible people lead their lives by logic, not dreams!

Interestingly enough, we only have two innate fears wired into us at birth. It doesn't matter what ethnicity or culture we were born into. Every baby is born with a fear of falling and a fear of loud noises. That's it. Every other fear has to be learned from living in this world. All these fears and anxieties begin to infect our hearts and turn us into what I call "Control Driven Men." We think that we can control our environment to protect our wounded hearts. In the short term, it tends to work. We all can typically find something or other that people will value us for – work, sports, school, clubs, confidence, jokes etc.

But when that something doesn't flow from the dreams that God placed in our heart, we will end up feeling a void in our lives.

That's why we see seemingly successful people drink too much alcohol, do drugs, or even commit suicide.

That's why every time I accomplished something, it was never enough.

How could it be "enough?"

How could I find fulfillment in something built without inspiration?

Think of the heart as inspiration and the mind as execution.

We need both.

When we execute without the inspiration coming from our own heart, we are implementing someone else's dream. This is not a problem if our heart aligns with the vision of the organization like a church, a non-profit or even a corporation.

But if our mind convinces us that the "adult" thing to do is to prioritize our boss or girlfriend over what our heart tells us, we become Control Driven Men. We are controlling ourselves into becoming someone who fulfills other people's expectations. People-pleasing will likely earn us approval in the short term but will come at the expense of distancing ourselves further from our unique calling.

There is an alternative – becoming someone I call a "Love Driven Man."

A Love Driven Man doesn't ignore his mind but instead uses logic as a tool to bring out the best in his heart. He knows that to accomplish something great, he will need a foundation of inspiration for the days when the going gets tough. In other words, a Love Driven Man understands that a correctly oriented heart will make all the difference, and that's why his priority is on developing a secure emotional connection with what's eternal.

God is that "eternal connection." He is the same yesterday, today, and forever. (Hebrews 13:8)

This long-term perspective is something that we often miss in our childhood. Often, our father figures do not inspire us to develop a personal relationship with God. Nor do they teach us how to execute our lives based on eternal truths.

Instead, our hearts become infected with fear of pain.

Consequently, our minds take control and try to minimize the amount of fear in our lives.

Control prevents us from taking action. When we face multiple choices, our mind gets worried about making the wrong decision, so we stick to the status quo. Continuing to do the same things gives us the certainty that we will not make a mistake, but it also deprives us of the upside. To make the decision calculations more straightforward for the part of us that wants a sense of control, I purposefully named chapters to help you think of just two outcomes. Much like a computer code that runs incredibly powerful systems such as the internet with only two options, 1 and 0, current or no current, I want you to focus on the basics:

THE LOVE DRIVEN MAN

Is the choice I'm facing going to make me more of a Control Driven Man or a Love Driven Man?

At first glance a Love Driven choice might seem too overwhelming to pursue. Don't make the perfect, the enemy of good. In the military, I learned that the best way to overcome indecision is to take action, however small or trivial that action might appear to be. Even a half step forward in the right direction is better than no step, or worse yet 20 steps in the wrong direction. So, each chapter will contain two action items that will help you see how simple the first steps towards your authentic identity can be!

At the end of each chapter, you'll find reflection questions. Please take some time to reflect on them before you move to the next chapter. Feel free to write down your thoughts in the book or better yet open a word processor document and start journaling the answers to the *"Reflection Questions."* These questions will help you to connect the book to your story. The personal connection is precious, because it will make it easier for you to spot opportunities to be a more loving person. More importantly, it will make it easier for you to take action. I also highly encourage you to discuss these questions with a spouse, friend, or mentor. As many people as you can! Please check out the Appendix B outline. I think you'll find it very helpful. These conversations will take your relationships to the next level, and you will gain insights from hearing another person's perspective.

Will Bowen famously said, *"Hurt people hurt people."*[1] This book will help you to break that cycle. When we control, we hurt other people, and ourselves. On the flip side, healed people can become an instrument of healing for other people. They are living testimonies of God's love available to all.

Our world revolves around control. Think about how many industries exist solely to control your image (i.e., luxury cars), disappointment (i.e., alcohol), and even free time (i.e., social media). It's all around us. Control shuts off our heart so that we start conforming to our temporary home in this world because we don't believe God has created us for a lot more.

The good news is that just as we learned to control from others, we can also learn to love from others. We just need to open our eyes to what's hidden in plain sight of our closed-off hearts. As you open up your heart more, you'll begin to see the downside of control, and you'll start looking forward to the upside of love. Not only will you break the cycle, but you will become the miracle you wish you had experienced when you were growing up.

You'll become a Love Driven Man.

Your example will inspire others to open up their hearts as well.

From an eternal perspective, what can be better than that?

Chapter 1: Your Godly Identity
Am I controlling people's perceptions or uncovering my own godly identity?

"For you did not receive the spirit of slavery to fall back into fear, but you have received the Spirit of adoption as sons, by whom we cry, 'Abba! Father!'"
Romans 8:15 (ESV)

A Control Driven Man wants people to admire him, which results in a need to control his identity to fit other people's expectations.

A Love Driven Man's goal is to cherish his personal identity in Christ, which helps him let go of any desire to control the uncontrollable and instead to grow in love for what matters eternally.

In this chapter, I'll explain the two most effective ways to uncover your godly identity – growth in prayer life and developing an emotional connection with the Bible.

I spent ten years working for ExxonMobil in project management. One of the key concepts I learned was, to begin with the end in mind. Oil and gas projects are super expensive. The ones I worked on were at least $5 billion. Some can cost as much as $60 billion. All projects, whether the facility was being planned to extract oil in deep water, a remote jungle, or even the arctic, would go through the 3 key phases: engineering, procurement, and construction. First, you would have to design the facility to meet the requirements in the engineering phase. Then, during the procurement portion of the project, you would need to purchase pipe to carry the crude and equipment such as pumps to move it. At the end comes the construction phase when you get out to the field and put everything together. Typically, all these stages combined take at least three years to finish.

Each phase becomes more expensive than the previous. You change the design only as a last resort! Let's say the requirements do change, and you need 12-inch pipes instead of 10-inch pipes. In the engineering phase, this change is not too bad – you simply allocate some extra engineering hours to redo the drawings. In the procurement phase, change becomes more expensive, because now you have to purchase and bring to the field a whole bunch of pipes you did not budget for. The worst time to make a change is in the construction phase because now you'd have to rip out the 10-inch pipe and install the 12-inch pipe from scratch. Not only is that very expensive in terms of labor, but the extra time needed for this rework will delay your start-up date. Since an average facility produces millions of dollars of oil per day, that's a big problem. Worse yet, buyers could cancel their purchase agreements and go somewhere else to get the crude.

The very same project management principles apply whenever I try to obtain approval to feel valued.

My initial identity specification came from an abusive grandfather. He kicked my dad out of the house and had me, my mom, and my grandma living in a constant state of fear. I couldn't do anything right. In fact, to this day, I still remember the tightness in my chest at his mere look of disapproval. The worst thing about my grandfather's criticism was that it came when I least expected it and it came typically over something that was very trivial.

> I remember one time when I was by a campfire grilling sausage on a stick. You know, because in Poland all we eat is

THE LOVE DRIVEN MAN

Polish sausage (I'm not helping the stereotypes here). The point is, I was having a good time with my friends when out of nowhere my grandfather started yelling at me for the way I ate my sausage: *"What's wrong with you! The way you eat is so greedy! Look at your friends – they are properly enjoying the sausage! Where did you get that from?"*

I felt like I wanted to disappear from the face of the earth. If I can't even eat a piece of sausage right, what **can** I do right?

The identity I got from my home was that *"There's something wrong with me."*

When I act *"wrongly,"* people criticize me, and I feel fear. I don't want to feel fear. I decided to control other people's perceptions of me so that my heart would not experience childhood pain again. That's one of the main reasons I decided to go to West Point. I figured that the military would take the "mistakes" out of me. I knew that the process would involve more yelling, but it would be worth it. For once I donned the Army uniform, I would become criticism proof, or so I thought ...

Just like an oil and gas project, it takes a while before you fully learn the long-term consequences of your choices. You might be making decisions that make perfect sense given the current circumstances, but over time they can result in a conflicted identity. You didn't know what you didn't know.

When we are young, we typically excel at something. For me, it was computer science. I liked it, and other people admired me for doing something they considered difficult. Therefore, I majored in it. I thought my Computer Science degree choice would make my professional career bulletproof.

When I left the service, I engaged a recruiting company that specialized in finding military members jobs in the corporate sector. I told them that I wanted an IT job where I could use my degree. They told me that I should aim higher. I should leverage my leadership skills to make my mark in corporate America. That played to my fear-based desire to control how people view me. I rationalized away. *"Well, it's been a while since I coded, and since I went to West Point, I **should** seek out leadership positions in Corporate America,"*

That's how I ended up at ExxonMobil. The pay was great, and it got better the more I conformed to the *"Exxon"* way. I volunteered for expatriate assignments. I spoke with passion about things I didn't much care for. I assumed it was good to work overtime to the point that I was bragging about it to others.

Exxon was an infatuation, not love. There's nothing like hard times to help you distinguish between the two. In 2015, we got punched in the face when the price of oil crashed. It went from $120 per barrel down to $27. People whom the company had promised employment for life got laid off. It didn't make it easier when Exxon attributed the layoffs not to the bad economic environment, but due to *"sub-par personal performance."*

The fact that nobody saw it coming shook me up. The rude awakening made it painfully clear to me that the only reason I had taken my job was because of the pay and the perceived job security. I had zero emotional connection to my job.

THE LOVE DRIVEN MAN

Back then, I thought, *"Hey, welcome to the real world. I'm a slave to what I controlled myself into."*

I had way more to lose than to gain by changing, so I thought I had to make the best of it.

I felt stuck.

My Control Driven brain didn't see any other way except to continue adjusting to my environment. To me, changing at that time would be like ripping out 10inch pipe to put in 12inch pipe – way too much effort and I would have to take a revenue cut. Too much of my identity was wrapped up in my paycheck. My bank account became my justification. When I looked at the balance, I told myself, *"Look what I accomplished grandfather, you were wrong!"*

Furthermore, every time somebody was overly critical of me, I'd cut them out of my life, because what did they know? I had to be right all of the time; otherwise, how could I have made this much money?

With my source of money threatened by the downturn, I was terrified. My source of justification could go *"Poof"* at any minute!

That's why a Love Driven Man cries out to God and says, as in the opening quote above, *"Abba! Father! Save me from living by the flesh! Help me to see as You see!"*

Because a Love Driven Man knows that what his mind sees and understands will pass.

Our brains are finite, so what we consider to be a long-term strategy is typically a lot shorter than we think, just like the unexpected downsizing at Exxon. That's why a Love Driven Man focuses on opening his heart to what matters eternally. What is eternal, and therefore infinite, will never fit into our limited brains. By focusing our heart on what is holy, however, we discover our eternal identity as sons of God (Romans 8:13-14). The sooner we embrace our identity, the sooner we unearth the unique abilities that God placed in us to execute our God-given mission.

There is no need to worry whether or not it's too late for a big transition. Our lives are NOT like oil and gas projects that have to hit rigid deadlines and minimize redesign to be successful. It won't matter whether you are too far into your life to change, because it won't be a change *per se*. It will be an upgrade! Keep in mind, His plan may have been for you pick up many specific life experiences before you change direction. Don't waste time trying to backward engineer yourself into someone that you're not. Instead, embrace the person God designed you to be from the beginning.

A great way to illustrate the importance of identity are feral children. Several confirmed cases exist of human children who were raised by animals and thus, adopted the behavior of the particular species who took care of them.

Consider a case referred to in the Russian media as "dog boy."[2] It seems that he was raised by a dog from the time he was three months old. He lived in a remote part of Siberia for seven years after his parents abandoned him. Andrei couldn't talk and had adopted many dog-like behaviors such as walking on all fours, biting people, and sniffing his food before he ate it.

When the authorities took him in, he was afraid of people, behaved aggressively and continued to sniff all his food before eating it. However, just two weeks after his arrival, he began to walk on two legs! The reintegration process continues. The boy can only communicate in sign language but has begun eating with a spoon, making his bed and playing with a ball.

Feral children show that simple human behaviors we take for granted, like walking with our hands by our sides are not automatic. If someone doesn't model for us how our identity looks at its finest, we will continue to default to the common denominator in our community. To make my point more visual, without proper guidance, spiritually, we'll end up walking on all fours, instead of straight up in the image of God.

How to uncover your godly identity #1:
Growth in the prayer life

We are all human and as such imperfect. Even if some of us had better parents than others, they were still far from perfect. That's why prayer is paramount. It opens up a channel of direct communication to our perfect Father.

From a Control Driven Man's perspective, prayer looks silly. Asking someone you've never seen for something or repeating the words of the *"Our Father"* prayer seem illogical. You're wasting precious time instead of actually solving your problems.

I used to have the Control Driven Man's view on prayer – that it was a waste of time. The crucial transition for me was understanding that prayer is not a *"spell"* or a *"wish request to a genie in a bottle."*

Prayer is giving God permission to mold me so that I can do HIS will. My intentions may appear selfless to me, but my finite brain can never comprehend the infinite, eternal God whose Kingdom is my real home. When I pray, I still have requests, but I never judge

God's love for me based on how well He brings MY will into fruition. Quite the opposite. Through prayer, I acknowledge that I will never be able to comprehend God's ways. Spiritually, I'm much like an unborn baby. Can you imagine explaining to a fetus what this world is like? An unborn child can't begin to understand the emotional pleasure of the beauty of a sunset, or the great joy of being deeply loved by another person. In much the same way, how can we possibly fathom everything that awaits us in eternity, and more importantly, what is needed to prepare us to get there?

Prayer, therefore, is an act of surrender.

It is an acknowledgment of my limitations and a permission for God to open my heart to what He designed me to do. There's nothing better than that. The only catch is that the Divine Intervention in our lives typically becomes apparent only when you look back. Newborn babies come out crying from the womb because they don't want to leave. Coming into this world is a traumatic event for them. Looking backward as an adult though, I haven't met anybody who wants to go back into his mother's womb!

Prayer is so important because it allows us to persevere when our desire to control, to point fingers, and most importantly to resist change tries to take over. A Love Driven Man understands that in this world, we can't do it alone. We are always placing our faith in something. For me, it was an ExxonMobil paycheck to provide for ALL of my needs.

Through prayer, I was able to endure the downturn calamity with peace because I learned to look past the turbulence, to Jesus. My mind didn't exclusively obsess on how to dig in deeper so I could weather the storm. The small periods of detachment from the fear of losing my job that came as a result of prayer allowed me to recognize that my season at Exxon had long passed.

Looking back, I realized that the downturn was the best thing that ever happened to me. It woke me up to my identity in Jesus Christ and gave me an opportunity to trust Him. I discerned that staying at Exxon would be My will, but moving on was God's will. Consequently, I quit the job I had held on to so tightly and started my own business. This was a leap of faith that I would not have taken had I not grown my prayer life.

Prayer is a great start.

The next step, to keep the fire rising, is building an emotional connection with something else that is eternal, the Word of God: the Bible.

How to uncover your godly identity #2:
Developing an emotional connection with the Bible

I took plenty of mandatory religion classes in Poland and later even more at my Catholic high school in California, but I didn't believe any of it.

Yes, I knew the rituals. I knew what it took to get an "A" on the test, but not the story behind it. In my mind, the Bible was a series of disjointed facts, which I would forget right after the test, so as to make space for yet another round of disconnected material. Since I didn't know the full story, I didn't develop an emotional connection with the Word of God.

It wasn't until I joined a Bible study group, that I finally understood that I couldn't read the Bible like a novel. The Bible is more like a library of different books, and so without a proper context, confusion is inevitable.

Instead of random chunks here and there, I finally read the Bible in a timeline sequence, which is very different from a page sequence. With the addition of a proper narrative, the full salvation story from Genesis to Revelation finally clicked! More importantly, I saw myself as part of the story that is still unfolding. I used to think, *"Man those Israelites that Moses led out of Egypt, what a bunch of morons! God did all these miracles – sending the plagues on the Egyptians, parting the Red Sea and providing manna in the desert – but they still wouldn't listen. They still wouldn't believe!"*

That's when the lightbulb went off.

I asked myself, *"How am I different from the Israelites?"*

There is so much in my life that's been miraculous, but I still didn't believe. I still required a miracle at every single turn. By getting to know the scripture better, I realized that my story echoes the Bible story. I used to open the Bible ONLY when someone at Church or school told me to do it.

Now I open the Bible when I need strength. More specifically, in that very same Bible study, I came across the following few verses from the book of Sirach. All these years later, I still go back to it whenever the part of me that wants to control feels disappointed:

[1] My child, when you come to serve the Lord,
  prepare yourself for testing.
[2] Set your heart right and be steadfast,
  and do not be impetuous in time of calamity.
[3] Cling to him and do not depart,
  so that your last days may be prosperous.

THE LOVE DRIVEN MAN

⁴ Accept whatever befalls you,
 and in times of humiliation be patient.
⁵ For gold is tested in the fire,
 and those found acceptable, in the furnace of humiliation.
⁶ Trust in him, and he will help you;
 make your ways straight, and hope in him.
⁷ You who fear the Lord, wait for his mercy;
 do not stray, or else you may fall.
⁸ You who fear the Lord, trust in him,
 and your reward will not be lost.
⁹ You who fear the Lord, hope for good things,
 for lasting joy and mercy.
¹⁰ Consider the generations of old and see:
 has anyone trusted in the Lord and been disappointed?
Or has anyone persevered in the fear of the Lord and been forsaken?
 Or has anyone called upon him and been neglected?
Sirach 2:1-10 (NRSVCE)

So find a course or group that resonates with you and learn from them. Even though you might think you know enough, trust me, you will discover that there is always another layer: a more profound mystery to uncover. That's how you'll build an emotional connection that will go beyond what might appear as outdated texts to our minds. The more you grow this emotional connection, the less you'll care about what others think, and the more you'll care about uncovering your godly identity.

Think about it.

We've all heard stories about the crazy things men do for women. I'm sure you have done something similar in your life! When you did it, did it feel like sacrifice? Did it seem crazy? Probably not, you did it because of an enormous emotional connection.

Now imagine developing that very same massive emotional connection with the Bible and consequently doing things that may seem crazy to others, but for you are second nature.

That's the goal! A hefty goal, but the closer you get to it, the more meaningful your life will become. So, keep growing that connection to the point that your love for God looks like an infatuation to others!

Conclusion

Identity is like wearing glasses. It boils down to just two choices.

When I wear glasses of control, fear controls me. As I try to manage what other people think, I end up conforming to what others expect of me. People's expectations change, and it's only a matter of time before I become unnecessary. The inevitability of my redundancy is tremendously stressful.

When I wear the glasses of Psalm 139:14 *"I praise you because I am fearfully and wonderfully made," (NIV)* I grow in my ability to love. As I become more open to God working through me, the questions of my inadequacy fade into the background. Yes, I fall short, but unlike people-pleasing, which is a moving target, now I make progress towards an eternal target. Even if the advance is slow, I know I'm moving in the right direction.

I don't have to worry if I'm wasting time or money on the wrong identity!

What a relief!

Chapter 1 Reflection Questions:

Where does your identity come from?

Do you let others see the real you, or do you carefully control how others see you?

Is your identity coming from God or your wounds?

How can you grow in your prayer life?

How can you build a stronger emotional connection with the Bible?

Chapter 2: Growing Closer to God
Am I seeking validation in accomplishments or in growing closer to God?

"Take delight in the Lord, and he will give you the desires of your heart."
Psalm 37:4 (NIV)

A Control Driven Man wants to earn people's admiration, which results in him having a focus on his accomplishments.

A Love Driven Man's goal is to grow in virtue, which brings him closer to God.

In this chapter, I'll explain the two most effective ways to build virtue – removing sin and putting yourself on God's timeline.

One day, I was scrolling my way through Facebook. I came across a video in which one of the most famous soccer players, Cristiano Ronaldo, disguised by a make-up crew, went out to practice at a city center plaza.[3] His juggling skills with the soccer ball were terrific, but no bothered to watch him. Even when Ronaldo went so far as trying to pass the ball to folks nearby, most looked at him like he was crazy. They rushed off even faster to their destinations. Only a passing kid took him up on the offer. They played together for a few minutes, after which Ronaldo took off his disguise and proceeded to sign his ball. With his mask off, everyone instantly recognized Ronaldo, and security had to be called in to help him get away from the crowd that quickly formed.

I began to wonder. *"Why did no one care when Ronaldo displayed the very skills that made him famous?"*

THE LOVE DRIVEN MAN

It was only after he showed his face and stopped playing soccer, that people started to pay attention!

Adults have a tendency to prefer what has been previously deemed by others as *"valuable."* In other words, we hedge our bets to make sure our choice is a *"safe choice."* Making our own decisions about value takes brain cycles and worse yet, our choice might not be approved by others in our environment, at least not at first. That's risky. Control Driven Men don't like risk.

Notice how a child was the only one who recognized Ronaldo's expertise. A Love Driven Child who didn't care about the worldly validation.

How does it happen? How could so many grow up and turn a blind eye to Ronaldo's actual soccer skills, but run towards his celebrity status?

The answer to these questions is essential because the same obstacles get in the way of us growing closer to God.

We crave prestige but overlook virtue.

Wounds in my childhood and teenage years left me searching in vain for healing through accomplishments. My journey in seeking the prestige started when I saw western commercials on TV for the first time. I grew up in communist Poland, where everything was minimalist and practical. Who cares about marketing if whatever you make has no competition?

When the Berlin Wall fell, we started seeing products from the *"west"* that looked like they came from a different planet. The merchandise was full of color. The packaging featured lots of smiles and excitement. Even a soap commercial made my jaw drop with awe. Believe it or not, I preferred watching ads to the Soviet-inspired programming! Over time, the TV advertisements lost their luster and became annoying, but in me, they planted an allure for shiny, out of reach objects.

Then there was the ultimate shiny object, the source of shiny objects themselves – the United States of America. *"What a fantastic place it must be,"* I thought. *"It has to be!"*

> When I watched American TV shows, everyone seemed so happy and when I watched sitcoms like the *Full House,* I saw kids adored by their parents. I wished that I had that! The US seemed like heaven. The contrast could have never been starker than when my grandfather would criticize my beloved shows. He'd say sarcastically, "American kids are such smart assess. They know everything. If only one of them could come over and be our president, we'd be wealthy like Americans in no time!"

I'd do my best to pretend that I didn't hear those comments and continued to smile as I longed for what I never experienced in my own life — **family love**.

I felt even more alienated after my dad passed away when I was ten years old. The sad thing was that I didn't even cry for him at his funeral simply because I didn't know him. Yes, I'd see him around, and I believe that he did his best, but I'd become too appearance-driven by then and my family did not look like the happy family on *Full House*. Ever since I could remember, my father lived with his parents and not with us. All of my peers' dads lived with them in the same house. Also, my grandfather hyphenated my last name, Rabkowski-Rudak, because he couldn't stand my dad and couldn't bear the fact that I would carry my father's name exclusively. None of my peers had a hyphenated name.

Most important of all, when he passed away, I was the only kid with a dead father. I was so ashamed of being different. I didn't understand that the purpose of a family is not to "look good," but to teach one another how to love. It's not just some *"organizational chart"* with all the positions neatly filled in.

My mom remarried when I was 13. Even though her new husband was Polish, he lived in the United States. I finally had an opportunity to move to the *"promised"* land. You'd think I'd be jumping up and down, but it wasn't so. I didn't want to go. I didn't notice it at the time, but now I know that this was the first instance in my life where even though I faced an opportunity for something better, I was too afraid of change. I didn't think I'd fit in. It's one thing to seek escape by experiencing what you want through other characters in a fairy tale. It's something else altogether to actually do it. I was an obedient child though, and I did what my family told me to do. I boarded the plane!

> I'll never forget the day my mom picked me up at the San Francisco airport. I looked at her coming my way, and I couldn't help but notice a huge belly. She was seven months pregnant! Nobody told me about that!
>
> At that moment, I instantly felt like a fifth wheel in my brand-new family. My mom had a new husband and a kid on the way. My dream of achieving the perfect family life in United States was crushed. *"What is my value? What am I bringing to the table?"*

My Control Driven brain made me feel redundant. I already felt like a misfit in Poland, but now it got even worse. I felt like my mom had a better, American, son on the way and it was only a matter of time before I got pushed out from the *"Perfect TV"* family. Just like my mom shocked me with her pregnancy, I imagined that she would shock me with my inevitable ouster.

So, I convinced myself that I needed to focus on my accomplishments because I couldn't rely on bloodline relationships. My logic was that if I earned good-enough grades, was accepted into a good-enough school, and had good-enough jobs, I could get control back and wouldn't have to rely on someone else's mercy.

Fear can be an excellent short-term motivator. That's what got me accepted to West Point. I was extremely proud and felt incredibly blessed. But, the Academy took the ideas that I had about accomplishments and elevated them to a whole new level. We were ranked on academics, physical training, and military performance. My class rank became my validation, and everything else faded into the background. The number one question for me at the time was: *"How is this going to improve my numbers?"*

> For example, one of the upperclassmen encouraged me to try out for the crew team. I tried it and enjoyed it. It was so relaxing to row on the Hudson River amidst the rolling hills, lush green colors and beautiful architecture sprinkled throughout, much like the stars that appear just after sunset. Participating in crew was so restorative. But then one day, the coach asked me to go on a trip to Princeton for a competition. I freaked out because I had a test and worried about missing out on the study time.

Consequently, I made up a story to miss the trip, and that was the last time I went to practice.

I have forgotten what the test was, but I'll always remember that I gave up on this opportunity for what I mistakenly thought was a higher validation opportunity.

Back then, I didn't view myself as a physically fit person. I felt that the only way I could make an impact was through academics. This memory helps me put my choices in perspective today, especially when I think back to my thirties when I started doing CrossFit. I discovered that I was a fantastic rower! Who knows what I would have accomplished if I had stayed with it decades earlier! More importantly, how much more would I have grown in virtue if I had that time on the water rowing to reflect on my life? Instead, I chose to overload myself with studying because I felt more in control.

I am glad that I joined the Army. As a Control Driven Man, however, I focused too much on the accomplishments. If I had to do it all over again, as a Love Driven Man, I would have focused more on growing virtue.

How to grow virtue #1:
Removing sin

Sinning is like cutting corners on a workout.

When you don't lock out your elbows or don't squat all the way down, you can typically accomplish more reps, but your fitness will suffer in proportion to how often you take shortcuts. Further, an incorrect form opens you up to injuries. You'll be tempted to add more weight than your muscles and joints are actually ready for. The proper way, much like virtue, requires patience and typically feels impossible early on.

Combat is all about winning.

Whether it was McArthur's *"There is no substitute for victory,"*[4] or *"You do what you got to do in time of war,"* that I was taught by some of my superiors or even the bluntest of them all, *"If you ain't cheating, you ain't trying,"* my key take away, as a Control Driven Man was, *"the end justifies the means."*

No, I don't mean doing anything illegal, just using the gray areas to my advantage to make sure that my self-proclaimed *"just causes"* have the highest chance of success possible. In other words, cutting corners, because doing everything by the book to win simply feels impossible.

> I think back to my experience in Ranger School. Ranger School is one of the toughest in all military training. So many people drop out on the first day that the instructors don't let you park in the parking lot until the afternoon. There's no way we'd all fit in. Future hopefuls like myself parked wherever we could find space on the sides of the road. It was chaos! After the fitness and water survival tests, whoever was still standing was finally allowed to move their car into the student parking lot. As I was driving my car in, I saw other guys on their cell phones. I was so proud of myself that I decided to call my mom to brag. Surprisingly my mom picked up! I don't remember what I said though, because the conversation was very short.

THE LOVE DRIVEN MAN

Out of nowhere, a Ranger Instructor started yelling at me: *"Get off your cell phone!"* He did that to a whole bunch of other guys. When I heard him scream, *"All of you on the cell phones, you will see me!"* I got super scared. I went from feeling extremely accomplished to worrying if I'm going home. Then I heard the internal voice of temptation: *"There's no way the instructor remembers me by name or face. There's hope!"*

Once we all got back from the parking lot, the Ranger Instructor told all the people on the cell phone to step out. Immediately I started rationalizing. Nobody told us not to use cell phones explicitly. So, I wasn't violating a direct order. Besides I remember reading a book about Ranger School in which the writer talked about a similar story. Except it was even worse. The Ranger Instructor misheard the writer's name, so when he called for Brailey, and his actual name was Bagley, the writer thought *"God really wants me to be a Ranger"* and didn't step out. In my mind, I was justified, so I stood firm. I was making a "manly" decision. That's what soldiers in wartime do!

But then I saw some of my colleagues step out. One of them I knew from West Point.

Part of me thought, *"I wish I had the guts to do that."* But my Control Driven side got the best of me, and I reasoned that I was making a better decision. Why risk graduation over something this trivial? I rationalized away that these guys were too idealistic for the Army. Even though I hadn't fought in war yet, I convinced myself that hiding to graduate was the kind of necessary decisions combat leaders have to make on the battlefield to secure victory!

> The guys who stepped out were the real heroes. The instructor knew that he had seen way more men on their cell phones, but enough stepped out to make him feel like we didn't blow him off altogether. The men who stepped out ended up getting minor punishments. I could have easily graduated with that.

I compromised my integrity for nothing.

And with each sin, however small it was, I moved farther away from virtue and consequently farther away from God.

Accomplishments became my god, and how I got there became an afterthought.

Now I realize that the means are more important than the ends.

Only Control Driven Men *think* they *know* what's best for them.

Love Driven Men know that what's best will come when they focus on giving greater glory to God.

Just like the way my exercising form is far more important than what my one rep max is on any particular day. If the Lord is pleased with our honest efforts, the result will always be better than our brains can imagine.

Consider friendship.

As a Control Driven Man, I looked for friends who made me feel good about myself. That's the end I had in mind. What this meant in practice was that I sought out people who validated my opinions.

THE LOVE DRIVEN MAN

Even though in my heart, I knew that gossiping was wrong, and that I drank too much, those means justified the ends. A "friend" who understood me meant someone I could complain with!

As a Love Driven Man, I focus on the means when it comes to friendship because I know that with quality friendships, the ends will surpass my expectations. I don't mean ends judged by worldly standards but by godly standards. In time, because I befriended people who put means over results, I decided to stop drinking alcohol, started fasting, began taking cold showers, and got inspired to follow through on my spiritual commitments.

All this together helped me root out sin and brought my heart closer to God. The result is my ability to see extraordinary things that are hidden in plain sight. The extraordinary is the eternal beauty that I regularly missed because sin had me looking in the wrong direction.

Drinking alcohol is a great example. I didn't drink very often, but when I did, I typically drank too much. I drank in social settings – in other words, places where I wasn't comfortable. I figured that drinking would help me to connect with people with whom a conversation would otherwise be uncomfortable.

Ironically, when I drank, the discussions were very uncomfortable, not for me, but for the people that had to listen to me! For example, I'd spill my drink, repeat myself, or insult people. It didn't happen every time, but the last time it did, my wife Jessi got upset and left the social gathering early without me. That was the final straw that broke the camel's back for me. I decided to quit alcohol. Being close to people who don't drink made the choice much more possible for me. Had I been in my previous circle of friends, the thought of quitting would have never crossed my mind because quitting alcohol would mean losing my friends.

And because I quit drinking, I got an opportunity to become a more loving person. Instead of running from discomfort in social settings, I get a chance to show up and learn how to build connections with people that my Control Driven brain told me I would never be able to connect with earlier.

Removing sin is putting God ahead of our earthly wants. If you feel overwhelmed, I want to reassure you that purifying your ways is a journey, not a destination. Even though you'll never be perfect, you can always be better. You'll know you're on the right track when you start experiencing more fruits of the Spirit in your life:

"But the fruit of the Spirit is love, joy, peace, forbearance, kindness, goodness, faithfulness, gentleness and self-control."
Galatians 5:22-23 (NIV)

A Control Driven Man will focus on how impossible it is to remove sin. A Love Driven Man will ask God for help and be thankful for the fruits of the progress, however small they may be.

How to grow virtue #2:
Putting yourself on God's timeline

The Control Driven Man also craves *"timing certainty."* Even now, when I do an ab exercise at a fitness class led by my wife, I do much better when I know how much longer I have to hold the pose. When I hold a plank on my left side, I see the timer on her cell phone, and I'm good. When I go to the other side, I get uncomfortable, and it feels like I'm doing the pose for twice as long.

THE LOVE DRIVEN MAN

That's how our minds work. Our brain wants us to make sure we know what to expect, so we don't waste our time. Or worse yet, run out of strength before we get the prize. I love the quote, by who I thought was Einstein, but from looking on the web, it isn't. Come to think of it, maybe it was accredited to Einstein precisely because that was the only way to make the idea famous – by giving it social validation! The quote is, *"Insanity is doing the same thing over and over again and expecting different results."*

The only non-renewable resource we can control is our time. You can always get more money, muscle, or even hair, but you can never get your time back. In other words, if you want to change, you have to understand your decision-making process because your choices got you to where you are today.

When I was at Exxon, I remember one of the instructors of the Contract Administration class said: "If you don't have time to make it right, what makes you think that you'll have time to do it over?"

From a legal perspective, it makes perfect sense. If you rush and don't talk through how the contractor's services will be delivered or worse yet, you sign the contract without reading it, you will spend exponentially more time reconciling the differences after the signature ink dries. That, in a nutshell, is why I should have never married my former wife. I rushed to get married without understanding what marriage is. Boy was it painful!

I sacrificed virtue to get the results faster. In other words, I wanted the benefits of marriage without wanting to spend the time to make sure I was ready for marriage. Marriage was yet another form of validation instead of an opportunity to get closer to God. As a

Control Driven Man, I didn't think I had the time. I had more important things to focus on.

I learned the hard way that *"rushing God"* **is** *"rushing to failure."*

Love Driven Men know that while they are on this earth, the question isn't *"when am I going to receive the prize, but am I ready to get the prize?"*

For when I ask myself, *"When am I going to get it?"* I start optimizing and looking for shortcuts. Grey areas begin to water down the means so that I can get the ends faster.

On the other hand, when I ask myself, *"Am I ready to get it?"* I focus on my heart. I realize that I can't do it on my own, so I ask God to help me out. I ask for the virtue of staying on His timeline.

The best example of that is my second marriage. When I met Jessi, my mindset wasn't how soon can I marry her, like it was with my first wife. My driving question became, *"Am I moving too fast?" "Am I ready to marry her?"*

Answering those questions required time spent in prayer. And through prayer, after weeks of discernment, I knew that this was the way to go. When we married, I didn't think, *"What took me so long?"* But rather I thought, *"Thank you God that you got me here."*

I knew that if we had met even a year sooner, we wouldn't have been ready for each other and our relationship would have collapsed under the weight of our closed-off hearts: our desire to Control.

By focusing on the means, over the ends, you are letting God recreate your time. My wife inspires me to get rid of bad habits like stuffing my emotions down and adopt good ones like praying each night before going to bed. The virtuous exchange gives me extra time to pursue the dreams that God puts into my heart. Something my Control Driven self could have never done on his own.

Conclusion

When it comes to validation, the best question to ask is, *"Where is your kingdom?"*

If your kingdom is on Earth, the Control Driven Man will always choose the most logical decision. It will be that which validates him the most in the court of popular opinion, or whatever are the current trends. Virtue shortcuts will look incredibly tempting through the lens of limited time on Earth.

However, if your kingdom is with God, a Love Driven Man will choose what delights God: that which is eternal. For even if it may not be the most logical choice at the moment, that choice will always bring out what matters most: a closer union with God.

Aspire for the virtues with eternal significance!

Chapter 2 Reflection Questions:

Where does your sense of worth come from?

Does it come from who you are, or what you do?

Is God your master, or are accomplishments your master?

What is your biggest sin? How can you start rooting it out of your life?

Think of a time when God's timing proved to be better than your timetable. How can you see more of God's timing in your life?

Chapter 3: Partnering with Women
Do I use women, or do I partner with women?

"Then the Lord God said, 'It is not good that the man should be alone; I will make him a helper as his partner.'"
Genesis 2:18 (NRSV)

A Control Driven Man wants a woman to make him feel better. He uses her.

A Love Driven Man's goal is to experience love at its fullest. He partners with her.

In this chapter, I'll explain the two most effective ways of experiencing love at its fullest. They are partnering with a woman who will help you follow God's will, and assuming positive intent.

Initially, the way I treated women came right out of my childhood home. I'll start with my grandmother because I spent more time with her than my mom while I lived in Poland. My mother became pregnant during her first semester in college. Grandma Helena was my physical mom, when my mother resumed her studies and later worked in Western Europe for months at a time.

> Ever since I can remember, my grandma was either catering to my grandfather's every need or yelling back at him when he was yelling at her. Nothing in between. There was no dialogue, no discussion — every conversation was binary. My grandfather looked down on my grandma. She was just a dumb woman in his eyes. I am ashamed to admit it, but I used to call Grandma Helena *"durna baba."* In Polish, that means "stupid woman." I don't remember it, but since that's

what my grandfather called my grandma, I must have picked it up from him.

I don't like to admit it, but the fact of the matter is that based on my upbringing, my general assumption was that all women were dumb.

> Interestingly enough, when I met my former wife, the nickname I used for her with my cousin was *"glupolek"* which roughly translates as "silly." My female cousins were even harsher. They called her "tic-tac" which comes from a commercial of a super small breath mint, referring to her brain size.

Again, I understand now how wrong I was to use those terms and even letting my cousins to come up with their own. Knowing what I know now, however, I am stunned by how natural it was for me to be biased against women. I had such a low opinion of a woman's intelligence that it is no wonder that brilliance was not a consideration when I was looking for a wife.

When it came to my mom, we never had a very close relationship. She always found a way, however, to make me feel special. The best way I can explain it is that we were both abuse survivors who never found a way to talk about the abuse.

Living with my grandfather was like living on a minefield. Except these landmines didn't tear your flesh. My grandfather's screams would tear into our sense of self-worth and after each blowup we'd feel more worthless. So my mother's giving nature was her attempt to deal with something neither of us ever healed from.

> For example, mom would send me letters when I was at West Point. Even though it was a whole bunch of fluff, I

looked forward to receiving them. Those letters became such a predictable place of refuge amidst the chaos of me trying to figure out what it meant to be a cadet. I'd say thank you for the letters, but I never let her know how much those letters meant to me.

She also sent me packages when I was in Iraq. I was deployed there in the first year of the war, so whatever I had, I either brought with me, or it was issued to me. There were no stores to buy things. Consequently, whenever I got a package, I felt like a kid at Christmas. I was excited to see what I had received. Again, I'd say thank you, but I never let her know how much those packages meant to me. Or when we talked on the phone, it was typically my mom asking me questions and me responding with a few, short sentences. Even though we experienced a lot of awkward silence, I loved talking to my mom, because I felt like someone cared that I was alive.

Unfortunately, I never told her that either.

Enter the second thing I picked up from my childhood home. I wanted to feel special but did not learn to express gratitude.

I can't overemphasize how embarrassed I am to admit it. But based on my upbringing, the Control Driven Man inside of me came to believe that a woman would never understand me. I thought they weren't smart enough. Accepting women's lack of intelligence as a fact led me to women who made me feel special. Oh, and by the way, when I found them, I didn't think I needed to express my gratitude.

What did it mean in practice?

You guessed it.

> I never even tried to connect with my first wife at a deep level because I thought she wasn't capable of appreciating my point of view. In the beginning, my former wife found ways to make me feel special. She wrote me letters (like my mom), sent me packages in Afghanistan (like my mom did when I was in Iraq) and called me to ask a ton of questions just to get short responses (like my mom).

Just as with my mom, I would say "thank you." but I was thanking her for doing what I expected her to do. I was *not* expressing my gratitude, because I wasn't grateful.

It wasn't long until the arguments started. My former wife would complain about me not doing enough work around the house, not wanting to go out, having too many routines, and even the fact that I liked to wear my old army t-shirts.

All of these gripes were absolutely true!

> In the last year of our marriage, while working for Exxon, I was on a rotational assignment to Nigeria – four weeks there, four weeks off in Houston. I preferred to be working in Nigeria because coming home stressed me out. I honestly thought that avoiding my first wife was normal. If you watch TV shows, who has a happy marriage? When was the last time you saw a movie in which a married couple demonstrated excellent communication skills? I thought that one of these days my then wife would understand what

I was doing for our family, but for now, I just had to settle for temporary misery. I thought to myself, *"It has to get better with time, right?"*

I continued to firm up in my beliefs that control is the way to go.

What's more, I thought that I was getting better at it.

I was using my former wife, because I expected her to conform to MY will.

I'll never forget a conversation with a Catholic Deacon who gave me a serious perspective changer. He told me that **a good marriage is the fastest way to heaven**.

At first, that struck me as a bit self-righteous. However, as I thought about it some more, I realized I'd get to heaven faster by becoming better at doing God's will. If I am with the right partner, much like a workout buddy, doing God's will, will become easier. Not easy, but easier.

This insight helped me to transition from a Control Driven to a Love Driven view of the women in my life. To put it even more plainly, I stopped USING women and started PARTNERING with women.

Probably the purest example of that is sex before marriage.

How to experience love at its fullest #1:
Partnering with a woman who will help you follow God's will

Love is a verb. So is Control. As a Control Driven Man, I settled for infatuations. I defined my manliness by how fast I was able to get a woman in bed. If I couldn't, I'd be upset. If I did, of course, it would feel exciting. However, once the feeling of excitement left, guilt set in.

I did what I saw in the movies and TV ads. I did what was supposed to make me happy. So, I stuffed that guilt down and enjoyed the infatuation while it lasted. When the relationship collapsed, I started looking for the next one.

To put it in ugliest words possible, I would not have married my former wife had I not practiced *"try before you buy."* I was using her as an object to satisfy MY urges. I rationalized away, by saying to myself that *"It's okay"* because *"I proposed to her."*

Unfortunately, since that's how our relationship started, it also continued into our marriage. A matrimony built on infatuation was not anywhere close to the foundation needed to endure the regular earthquakes caused by the tectonic plate friction of our mismatched expectations.

I wanted to avoid my prior mistakes in my second marriage. When Jessi asked me if I was willing to avoid all sexual contact until we were married, as a man who wanted to be more Love Driven, I said, *"Yes. Of course!"*

However, if you had pulled me off to the side back then and asked me if we would follow through, to be honest, I would have to say we would eventually slip. But it would be okay because that's just not a realistic expectation for a couple in their mid-thirties. We know better than younger couples anyways. It would be good enough. At least we tried!

By the grace of God, we did persist! There were trials, but interestingly enough, when I got weak, Jessi was strong and vice versa. Even though the commitment was way harder on me, and there were many times when I got upset, it was indeed a team effort. I even remember one time, when I surprised myself and I pulled us both away from compromising. As lopsided as it was, we couldn't have done it on our own, but together we helped each other to meet a seemingly impossible commitment. That experience became a basis for us becoming helpers and partners for each other in doing God's will in our lives. And it just got better and stronger in our marriage.

By the way, if you are already married, it's never too late to start making changes wherever you are at! It just takes God and effort to be partners.

Partnering with a woman to help each other get closer to God is a fantastic starting point. It's like having an impressive engine with great potential. But for that engine to work correctly, you have to feed it with proper fuel. That fuel is communication.

How to experience love at its fullest #2:
Assuming positive intent

As a Control Driven Man, I acted like people could read my mind. When they didn't, I'd either blame them or assume there was something wrong with me. Whenever conflict started, it would typically be the beginning of the end. Arguments would start a wedge that would only grow bigger and more painful over time.

However, as I became more Love Driven, I realized that conflict could be a fantastic relationship enhancer; with proper communication skills, of course!

The movie scene that brought it home for me came from Matrix Reloaded.[5] Neo, the main character, wanted to speak to the Oracle. When Neo went into a room where he thought he'd find the Oracle, he saw a mysterious man instead who said:

"You seek the Oracle. My name is Seraph. I can take you to her, but first, I must apologize."

"Apologize for what?" Neo responds with a surprise

"For this" Seraph replies as he attacks Neo.

An intense 1-minute kung fu fight scene ensues, which ends with Seraph holding up his hand and saying:

"Good. The oracle has many enemies. I had to be sure that you are the one."

"You could have just asked," replies Neo.

"No, you do not truly know someone until you fight them."

I'm not an advocate of fighting. The fact of the matter is, we are imperfect, and therefore, fights WILL happen. During those fights, however, we always have a choice.

We can grow in fear that we're losing control, or we can grow in love by respecting our partner and getting to know this person better.

As a Control Driven Man, I assumed **harmful intent** on the part of the other person. This assumption resulted in anxiety. This is fear that *"Here is yet another person who doesn't get it."* Or *"There's something wrong with me because I can't articulate myself in a way that convinces the other that **I am right**."*

Of course, the right views were always MY views.

THE LOVE DRIVEN MAN

As a Love Driven Man, now I believe in **positive intent**. I assume that the people I get to meet every day are doing the best they can. The conflict then becomes an opportunity to understand their perspective better and quite possibly recalibrate mine. The fact that they get upset or decide to fight back indicates that their viewpoint is important enough to risk a painful clash.

> One day, I got upset with my wife, because she told me to be careful when tucking in the footrest on my recliner. Jessi was worried that our cat, Nolan, might get hurt. To me, that was so improbable that I felt as if my wife was picking on me like my grandfather did when I was younger. I assumed harmful intent, and things went downhill from there. I got angry inside and defaulted to my version of an epic *kung fu* fight: the silent treatment.

Praise the Lord, that by this point in our union, I realized that I didn't want to repeat the broken patterns of my first marriage.

> I decided to assume Jessi had a positive intent and initiated a conversation later on that day. Yes, initially it was very awkward to share that something this seemingly trivial had upset me. I was also a bit worried that we'd end up talking past each other and that this conversation would damage our relationship further. I ended up being very glad that we talked about it.
>
> Jessi shared with me that her being overprotective of her animals went back to her childhood. Her parents didn't pay enough attention to her well-being, and that's why she wanted to give her animals something that she wished she

had gotten more of as a child. My wife, on the other hand, was surprised by how deeply my grandfather had hurt me.

Our decision to stop elevating the conflict allowed us to get to know each other at a deeper level, and our conversation resulted in healing.

Assuming positive intent frees me to explore how a different person sees the same issue from a different angle.

On the flip side, when I assume harmful intent, my viewpoint is locked. I'm essentially forcing the other person to see the issue from my vantage point, even though their unique life path placed them at an entirely different viewing location. In other words, when I assume harmful intent, there is no way they can see the same thing I'm seeing unless I can adequately paint my viewpoint and meet them where they are.

Further, by assuming positive intent I realized not only how smart my wife is but also began to see how smart other women were too. I learned that the only reason I used to assume women were stupid, was because I didn't want to hear what they had to say. It was too true for me to handle!

Conclusion

Back in 1999, NASA lost a $125 million Mars orbiter because a Lockheed Martin engineering team used English units of measurement while NASA's team expected the numbers to be in the metric system.

Interestingly enough, the unit mismatch wasn't the root cause for the accident. A NASA official stated: "This is an end-to-end process problem, a single error like this should not have caused the loss of Climate Orbiter. Something went wrong in our system processes in checks and balances that we have that should have caught this and fixed it."[6] In other words, there should have been enough fail-safes between NASA controls and the orbiter to prevent the crash.

This example shows the importance of not only communicating in the way that each of the two parties will understand what the other is saying (English vs. Metric system) but also having the ability to handle the times when the two parties are talking about the same thing but in languages that are incomprehensible to each other.

A Control Driven Man will assume that a woman will never understand him, and the relationship will blow up, like the Mars orbiter.

A Love Driven Man, on the other hand, will do his best to partner with a woman who talks in the same "measurement" system. Even when miscommunication happens, the relationship will not explode, as the couple will have enough goodwill NOT to give up until the message is properly delivered and correctly received.

Amazing goodwill comes from a couple's commitment to experience love in its fullest. However, messy or lengthy the communication process might be, when the two get there, the accomplishment will always be well worth it.

Even better than landing on Mars, a successful partnership with a woman gives us a foretaste of the eternal love we are all looking for!

Chapter 3 Reflection Questions:

Does your romantic partner (past or present) say things to you that imply she doesn't understand you? How often?

Are you able to be honest with your romantic partner, or are there things that you are hiding (past or present)?

Are you asking God for help, or are you passively waiting for changes in your relationship (past or present)?

What can you change in your relationship so that the two of you help each other get closer to God? If you are single, apply it to your relationship search.

How can you leverage the inevitable conflict to get closer to each other? If you are single, apply it to your relationship search.

Chapter 4: Transforming the Pain
Am I covering up the past
or letting God transform the pain?

"So if anyone is in Christ, there is a new creation: everything old has passed away; see, everything has become new!"
2 Corinthians 5:17 (NRSV)

A Control Driven Man wants to be perfect, which results in covering up the past.

A Love Driven Man lets God transform the pain from the past to open up his heart towards the future.

In this chapter, I'll explain the two most effective ways to shed the chains of the past – making discomfort enjoyable and using envy as a hint.

I grew up admiring perfection.

It's as if by adoring perfection, I daydreamed away my imperfections and disappointments. I told myself, *"I know that I am far from perfect, but by idolizing perfection, at least I am not settling for the status quo. I am doing something about it!"*

The problem is that I was chasing a mirage: something fake. And worse than that, the chase was a downward spiral. The more I fell short, the more I felt stressed. The more I felt stressed, the more I was prone to falling short. This vicious cycle assured that my past kept poisoning my future.

Take, for example, my earliest *perfect* hero: Napoleon Bonaparte. Just about everyone would agree that he was one of the world's most successful military commanders. Many would even say that he was the best. I thought, *"Wow, if I could be just like him!"*

But the gap between where I was in my life, and his accomplishments couldn't be more extreme. I thought his success was genetic, and so I often wished that I had been born like him. The comparison made me resentful. *"Why wasn't I born with the same exceptional skills?"*

Bonaparte had skills such as his multitasking ability. As an Emperor, for example, Napoleon would often arrange a dozen secretaries around him and dictate a dozen letters simultaneously. Because I focused so much on Napoleon's seemingly perfect abilities, I didn't learn until much later that his brilliance actually became a liability.

The leaders of the world powers of his time were afraid of his success and formed multiple alliances to defeat him. They couldn't fathom that a person NOT born into the royal aristocracy could become an Emperor. Napoleon fought them hard and overcame them in spite of insurmountable odds. This track record of epic victories eventually led him to invade Russia, where even his military genius could not overcome the harsh winter conditions.

My Napoleon envy is an excellent representation of how I tried to cover up my past. Since my grandfather's criticism infected my sense of self-worth, I craved the god-like skills that I thought Napoleon possessed. I wanted the kind of skills that would cause everyone to either respect me or be at the very least afraid of me. That was perfection to me: the ability to control what others thought about me.

Ironically enough, I missed the fact that even if I got those skills, I would still face defeat. After all, Napoleon lost everything because he became arrogant. He thought that he was better than all the others and didn't need to invest in relationships. For example, he started ignoring solid advice, even when it came from those whose advice he had respected in his earlier years. For him, it was much easier to bulldoze over nations with his military might. But the moment Napoleon stumbled, just about every foreign power turned on him.

The Control Driven Man inside of me thought that if I aimed for perfection, I would still be better off when I fell short than if I didn't try at all. The problem wasn't perfection, *per se*. The problem was that my lust for perfection had me running away from my real problem.

I didn't want to deal with the pain of failure — my real weakness. Instead of taking the time to learn why I felt that pain, I figured the best thing to do was to go full force on my next endeavor. I focused on achieving the next accomplishment because I thought that when I ticked off enough boxes on my checklist, they would cumulatively cover up the pain of my previous disappointments.

> By age 30, I thought I was making pretty good progress. I had just wrapped up an overseas assignment in Nigeria, and I was ready to start having kids. Having children was the next item on my checklist so that I could create something I never experienced myself - a happy family. I thought, *"My pursuit of perfection is finally paying off!"*

I was making way more money than I ever imagined, and I was confident that my kids were going to get everything that I lacked when I was growing up. In other words, all the pain that I had experienced would be foreign to them. I remember going on a run and smiling as I thought about how everything is finally coming together. As a Control Driven Man, I was delighted.

> Except that the last thing in the world, I expected to happen, happened. I'll never forget the night my former wife admitted that she was cheating on me with her boss. It was like a bomb went off.
>
> I was so shell shocked that I kept repeating "Jesus Christ, Jesus Christ."
>
> I couldn't believe that this was happening. She kept screaming, "What did you expect? You kept leaving me for your business trips to Nigeria!"
>
> My life could become an episode of the Jerry Springer show. As bad as it was, it seemed like every week I would find out something worse. For example, the guy lived in my house when I was in Nigeria. Later his wife told me that he was a serial cheater. What's more, during his last cheating episode, the husband of the wife with whom he cheated had committed suicide.

COMMITTED SUICIDE!!!

I knew some guys cheat, but women!!!

Especially with a guy who contributed to someone's death!!!

My life crashed because I firmly believed that all my accomplishments should have guaranteed me love.

Here I was just past my 30th birthday feeling like my life was over. I thought if a person this close would leave me, who would ever find me loveable? This whole experience was so overwhelming that I requested a work assignment in Angola. I wanted to disappear from the face of the earth. I wanted to protect my heart by running away from the pain.

When it came to physical fitness, I understood that I had to seek the burn to get better. I ran faster. I lifted heavier weights to tear my muscles up so that I could transform myself into a stronger person. In fact, as someone who did CrossFit for many years, I enjoyed tough workouts. But when it came to emotions, I didn't intuitively understand how similar my perceptions are to my muscles. I expected superior emotional transformations without significant discomfort.

How to transform pain #1:
Making discomfort enjoyable

However, I didn't always understand fitness. I was a chubby kid who loved sports but hated embarrassing myself. Consequently, I would participate, but only if I could protect myself from failure. A good example is how I approached dodge ball. I would hide behind the other kids and would never touch the ball. I was too scared to stick out. In my mind, I did *"good enough."* I participated, and because I was good at hiding behind people, I was typically one of the last ones to get eliminated. However, my defensive approach stunted my growth, because I never mustered the courage to pick up the ball, take a chance, and go on the offense. I was too scared to fail.

I had an innate desire to challenge myself, but no one showed me the way to do it, and I was too scared to figure it out on my own. My physical fitness turned a corner when a family friend, Mike, asked me if I wanted to go for a run with him. I agreed.

Now keep in mind, that I was the guy who would try to get a note from my grandma in Poland saying that I was sick so that I wouldn't have to do a 1 km run for Physical Education. I didn't want to be the last guy in my class. I avoided running like a plague because I didn't want to re-experience past failures.

The difference, though, was that Mike invited me to run with him. It felt nothing like a test that I might fail. We didn't have a specific route or even use a stopwatch. We just ran, and I felt so proud of myself afterward. I had to repeat it. Mike showed me how simple running was. His example made discomfort enjoyable. Just put on shoes and run through the parks across the street. I forgot about my past performance and started enjoying the very activity that used to terrify me. I looked forward to the discomfort because I knew that I would always feel better afterward! I went from avoiding running at all costs to missing it if I didn't do it for more than a few days; from being the last guy to a top tier finisher in my peer group at the local races.

Physical fitness was a massive step in the right direction, but it wasn't until I started yoga that I learned to enjoy something even more uncomfortable: trusting myself.

Yoga was yet another workout that took me a long time to try. Much like running, I was afraid to fail, because I was super inflexible. It's not even that I couldn't touch my toes. I could barely reach my knees! One day, my CrossFit coach mentioned to me this weird stretching workout called "hot yoga," and for some reason, I just knew that I had to try it.

THE LOVE DRIVEN MAN

You'd get a good laugh out of watching me doing the first class. I had no idea what was going on, fell a lot, and the instructor had to help me grab my legs for some of the poses. Even though the heat made me hyperventilate at times, I felt extreme relaxation when the class was over. As awkward as I felt attempting yoga, I wanted more!

The cool thing about hot yoga is that we did the same poses every time, so I could easily see the progress. Yes, it was slow, but that made the learning all the more powerful. I realized that yoga was not so much a flexibility work out as a mind-body connection exercise. The posture that best exemplifies my learning is the Dancer's Pose.

As you see from the picture above, the pose is all about balance. Yes, flexibility helps to get closer to the ideal, but it's the balance that underpins how far you get in the posture. At first, I tried to micromanage my muscles into a perfect, machine-like performance. The problem with this approach was that I was so focused on what I thought the pose should look like that when gravity kicked in, I couldn't compensate fast enough. Consequently, I fell over fairly quickly. Then I started to feel my way into the pose by letting the pose *"happen."* More specifically, every time I began to worry about falling over, I rechanneled the focus to my breath. It helped for sure!

However, I achieved a whole new level of mastery by doing something counterintuitive. I started to expect and looked forward to the balance struggle. Before, I tried to block out the fear of failure through breathing techniques. Now, I welcome the struggle to balance. Consequently, I rarely fall out.

In the past, even with the calming breath, I would accept that I did my best and fall over with peace. Now, I enjoy the process of getting back to the balanced state and as such leverage more muscles that I assumed had to be locked out to stay still earlier. The discomfort became enjoyable.

Looking for the balance struggle in yoga resulted in me doing great in a seemingly impossible pose. The process that helped me is just as applicable to something else that I considered out of reach: Love.

Love is welcoming discomfort as a teacher who shows us what we need to transform so that we can get closer to the eternal, God.

The Control Driven Man inside of me covered up discomfort because I took it as a sign that I wasn't measuring up. Whether it was running, yoga, or the fact that my former wife cheated on me.

The transition into a Love Driven Man happened when I stopped worrying if I measured up. Instead I began to enjoy the transformation of the past that polluted my heart.

The emotional equivalent of a physical workout in my life is *"Journaling."*

THE LOVE DRIVEN MAN

I journal every day which means nothing more than writing down what I liked or didn't like about the previous day. One major benefit comes from naming what specifically bothers me.

Whereas before I used to stuff bad feelings down and cautiously enjoy the good ones while they lasted, journaling allows me to understand what drives my emotional state. Rather than avoiding my feelings like I used to avoid running or yoga, I enjoy the daily discomfort assessment. I look forward to learning from what used to embarrass me.

There's tremendous power in knowing the enemy. For example, the American Coalition took over Iraq and Afghanistan in about a month when the adversary wore uniforms. However, once the war turned into an insurgency, and the enemy fighters mixed in with the population, the most powerful armies in the world became crippled. The coalition forces had the world's most potent weapons but very little idea who to aim them at. Consequently, the war in Afghanistan, which began in 2001, was still going on at the time of publication of this book, with no end in sight.

Similarly, before journaling, I wasn't able to identify my enemy. No wonder I wasn't making any progress!

An excellent example of the power that comes with knowing your biggest foe is the FBI's "Most Wanted List." The idea behind it is surprisingly simple. Just list the fugitives who are particularly dangerous menaces to society, then use nationwide publicity to help catch them. The results are astonishing! At its 50th anniversary, of the 458 fugitives listed, 429 have been apprehended or located.

The success comes from the FBI communicating to the public its priorities. If the FBI publicized a list of *everyone* they want to catch, it would be too much for the average person to wrap their mind around. Consequently, more criminals would have remained hidden in plain sight. Just posting the pictures and names of a handful made it impossible for these guys to remain at large.

Similarly, through journaling, I found my emotions' "Most Wanted List," at the top of which was intimacy. By taking about 5 minutes a day to write about how my previous day went, I gained tremendous insights. Through journaling about my bad dates, how people pissed me off, or how my career was stalling, I realized that beneath the drive for perfection was an unfulfilled desire for intimacy. I wanted to have relationships where I could be real, rather than having to cover up the parts of me that that I assumed others *might* find unappealing.

The very discomfort of writing about my pain and frustration led to the development of my first intimate relationship, the relationship with myself.

The more I became real in my journal, the easier it became to talk about what's really on my heart with others. The more I spoke about my pains, the more I realized that plenty of people around me share similar experiences. The more I talked with them, the more I was able to find and bring quality friends into my life.

Friends like my future wife, Jessi.

I'll never forget how Jessi opened up about her struggles in my small group at a retreat for people in transitions. The old, Control Driven Man inside of me would probably have labeled her as somebody with significant life issues who needs to clean up her act like a proper adult. However, as a Love Driven Man, I thought to myself *"I need to get to know her."*

She is somebody with whom I can have an honest conversation. I just wanted to get to know her. Much like a workout buddy, by talking to each other, I knew that we'd be able to transform our past as we found joy in talking about what we both had previously considered to be uncomfortable topics.

The more satisfaction I got from exploring my past; the more I grew. The more I grew; the more of a new creation I became. By walking through the discomfort, the shame of the past lost its grip. I was free to become more of what God wanted me to be.

But my growth bumped into another obstacle: envy.

How to transform pain #2:
Using envy as a hint

Whenever I compare myself to how I used to be: I am impressed. For example, in the first year after my former wife's affair, my first thought after waking up each day used to be resentment. Now I can't remember the last time I had any type of angry feeling first thing in the morning.

However, whenever I saw somebody I thought was doing better than me, I'd feel disappointment. I would wonder if my steps of courage into the pain were all worth it. Was I playing a game of *"whack a mole?"* I slowly transformed the pain, but I wanted validation. What's the point if whatever wound I'm healing is going to be replaced by another one? In other words, whenever I came across anybody who made me feel envious, I'd start questioning, *"Do I believe in what I am doing?"*

A good example from my life is public speaking.

When I first moved to the US, I was ashamed of my accent. I spoke as little as possible. Typically I would only speak if someone asked me a question. Avoidance worked until I went to West Point. At the academy, not only did I have to speak, but many of my instructors graded us on class participation. Since I was a sucker for good grades, I forced myself to talk more often. I was doing okay until my senior year. Just before graduation, I had to present to a group of peers on some trivial topic I can't even remember.

> I will never forget the first time it happened. I had never experienced anything like it. My body tensed up, my lungs deflated, and worst of all, my voice started cracking. I had no idea where it came from because the presentation wasn't even that big of a deal.
>
> Unfortunately, this wasn't an isolated incident. The anxiety attack became the new normal any time I had to speak up in a group setting. I was so embarrassed because I was a West Point graduate. Presenting should be natural to me! That's a big part of the reason I went to West Point. I wanted to communicate with confidence. However, my anxiety attacks were a huge step backward.
>
> Later, the embarrassment got even worse, as a highly paid Exxon Mobil employee. I deliberately avoided opportunities to present because I was worried that my management would call me out for being a fraud. For being unable to do what they had hired me to do, influence people with my communication skills.

THE LOVE DRIVEN MAN

As I continued to dig into my past, God began transforming the pain, and I became more of a Love Driven Man. I expected this anxiety to go away, but it didn't. It wouldn't budge, because the Control Driven portion of me had a fixed expectation of what I was going to do with "proper" speaking skills. That fear infected the part of my heart that wanted me to become so good at speaking that I would get a promotion. As I got real with myself, I realized that I was envious of my peers who weren't afraid to communicate in front of management. I'd called them *"sellouts"* at the time, but in reality, I was covering up for my resentment that I couldn't speak without anxiety.

Envy is a hint towards a higher calling. God placed the dream of speaking into my heart, and I didn't know how to apply it. I had to be patient. The Control Driven Man in us doesn't like patience.

Then one day, I was invited to speak about Eucharistic miracles to some people at a church. I was intimidated, but since the talk was short, the group small and I could read it from a paper, I thought I could stumble through it. But then the most exciting thing happened! When I shared my story, people responded. For the first time in my life, I wasn't afraid if I was good enough or not. I got excited when people visibly connected with what I was saying. They'd look me in the eyes, nod and say *"Amen!"* Even my sister, who just happened to be in town, and doesn't go to church on her own, enjoyed it and gave me props. She was the first person to tell me that I should have a podcast!

That's when I realized that my Control Driven self was onto something. I wanted to speak, but the purpose behind the pull needed to change to align with what God wanted me to do versus what I thought I should be able to do. As subsequent opportunities came up to speak, I took them up. The more comfortable I got, the smaller the fear of speaking became. Until about two years later it disappeared altogether. Yes, I still get anxious, but it's driven by excitement to connect rather than fear of failure.

Conclusion

Rock stacking seems like an impossible feat. Can you believe that the rocks below use nothing but gravity to remain in this position!

One day when I was scrolling through my phone, I saw a picture similar to the one on the right and clicked. I saw a video about Michael Grab, a stone balancing artist who shared the secret of how he learned to make these gravity-defying creations.[7] His approach was surprisingly simple: do it and not think about it. He started with making tall towers and stacking rocks from biggest to smallest. After doing that enough, he began to notice nuances that allowed him to take it further and further each time.

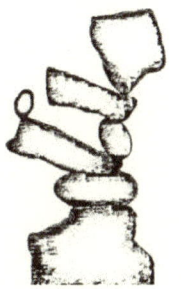

Transforming pain that stems from our past sometimes appears impossible as stacking a reality-defying rock arrangement. Even though the healing feels like mission impossible, don't let your mind talk you out of it. With God anything is possible.

For example, when the stone balancing artist thinks about the next steps too much, the rocks collapse, and fingers get broken! Stop overthinking! Be open to opportunities that you feel are uncomfortable.

THE LOVE DRIVEN MAN

In God's appointed time you will start noticing the joy that comes from your growth. When that growth feels insufficient as compared to someone else, you know you're on the right path. It's just a matter of finding a higher calling for the skills that you desire — a mission that will open your heart to what matters eternally and as such overshadows envy. It is God transforming that envy into self-confidence!

You'll know when you find it because the pain will fade into the background, and the fruits will give you a foretaste of the eternal.

Chapter 4 Reflection Questions:

What happened in your life that caused you a great deal of pain?

Are you offering up your pain to God, or are you running from it?

Is Jesus your healer, or did your mind declare that the pain is "incurable"?

How are you making the discomfort of growth enjoyable?

What makes you envious? What is the envy telling you?

Chapter 5: Taking Steps of Faith
Does my mind have the final say,
or do I give God space to work miracles?

"Trust in the Lord with all your heart, and do not rely on your own insight. In all your ways acknowledge him, and he will make straight your paths."
Proverbs 3:5-6 (NRSV)

A Control Driven Man makes decisions based on what he sees, which results in giving his mind the final say.

A Love Driven Man takes steps of faith to see more of God's Hand in his life.

In this chapter, I'll explain the two most effective ways to take steps of faith – giving time without expectations and relying on God for results.

During the War of 1812, British Major General Isaac Brock and the Shawnee Chief Tecumseh captured Detroit without so much as firing a single shot. Their American opponents outnumbered them and were protected inside a tactical fortification. General Brock knew from his experience that an attack would be very costly, and would use up resources he couldn't replace. A siege would take too long. So instead he and Chief Tecumseh prepared an elaborate bluff.

The bluff began in August when Brock besieged a 2,500-strong American force led by Brigadier General William Hull at what used to be called Fort Detroit. Even though General Brock had a much smaller army consisting of 300 regulars, 400 Canadian militiamen, and 600 natives, he more than made up for it through his ability to deceive.

Knowing that Hull believed the Native Americans to be ruthless barbarians, Brock allowed him to intercept a false letter indicating the British had 5,000 natives at their disposal. The British general then wrote a letter to the American general cautioning that his native force was so large that nobody would be able to control their bloodlust once the fighting started. He said he wouldn't be able to prevent a general massacre. While Hull was thinking this over, Tecumseh marched the same group of killer-looking and sounding natives past the fort multiple times to make his force look bigger and more savage. But General Brock didn't stop there. He clothed the Canadian militiamen in discarded British uniforms to make the Americans think they were up against significantly more deadly British veterans.

Faced with the cleverly coordinated mind game, General Hull lost his nerve and surrendered. It took the American Army more than two years to recover from a string of defeats such as this one and bring the war to a successful conclusion in 1815.

General Hull fell for the appearances. He allowed his mind to have the final say, which rendered his numerical and tactical advantages useless.

Similarly, as I look back at my romantic relationships, I realize that I allowed my mind to talk me out of taking steps of faith. I didn't believe I could find true love. Consequently, I endured a lot of pain, and my potential remained dormant.

For example, I wanted to find a *"good"* Christian woman, and I wanted her to be attractive. Based on my experiences, however, I came to believe that I couldn't find both. The *"good"* Christian girls weren't beautiful enough for me. So typically, I would go for the looks, and whenever I fell short, with having premarital sex or drinking too much, I didn't take ownership. I rationalized away that the woman made me do it, just like Adam blamed Eve for handing him the forbidden fruit in the Garden of Eden.

I had an inkling that I needed to go therapy.

At first, I resisted the idea. When my former wife mentioned going to the counselor, I felt insulted. I thought I was *"smarter"* than the people who needed it. However, when I started having suicidal thoughts after I found out my former wife was cheating on me, I knew I had to do something. The multitudes of briefings I received in the Army on suicide came back to me, and I decided to give therapy a try. Further, I didn't want to pass up on free divorce counseling offered by my employer.

I had a good experience that helped me get over the stigma of seeing a *"shrink."* So when I started seeing the repeating misery in my dating life, I decided to give therapy another try.

Through therapy, I found out that I was a codependent, which is also known as *"relationship addiction."* People with codependency often form relationships that are one-sided, emotionally destructive, or abusive. When my therapist diagnosed me as a codependent, I got angry. "What? .... Lady, Didn't I tell you that I was in the Army? I'm not a pushover, all right!!!"

However, once I calmed down, I started connecting the dots. They led back to my family home.

> My grandma, mom, and I bent over backward to make excuses for my grandfather, all the while, pretending that everything was peachy. The memory that brought it home

for me was hearing my grandma and grandfather argue in the hallway. My mom was with me in another room and did her best by turning to me and trying to make it sound like a joke. She said, "Oh look, your grandparents are just playing around like usual ... they're so funny, aren't they?" with a forced smile on her face.

Even as a kid, I sensed something was wrong. Especially when a few seconds later, my grandparents started to kick each other, and my mom ran out of the room to separate them.

Opposites do attract!

The opposite of a codependent is a narcissist, which just so happened to describe all the women in my past romantic relationships. I was drawn to the confidence which narcissists project. I was over the moon with their charm but ultimately always felt disappointed, because whatever I did was never enough in the long term. What kept me coming back was the euphoria of the first few months with a narcissist, also referred to as the *"love bombing"* phase. I was in heaven and felt like I had found *the one*! When a relationship with a narcissist soured, as it always did, around the three-month mark at the latest, I blamed myself. Just the way I blamed myself in my childhood home for my grandfather's narcissistic behavior.

I concluded that this was just the way my emotional wiring worked. I couldn't help being addicted to narcissists. Much like General Hull in the opening story, I kept seeing partners who confirmed my belief that love hurts.

My mind was entirely in charge, and it sought dysfunctional relationships.

That's all I knew. I didn't trust God to lead me to a better place.

How to take steps of faith #1:
Giving time without expectations

Another way to describe a codependent person is *"people pleaser."* At the surface level, the desire for others to be happy with me appeared noble. However, the unintended consequence of this seemingly innocent ambition was an expectation that whoever I spent time with, had to make me feel valued. I had a big attention void from childhood that would pull me towards toxic partners. At the same time, it would push me away from building healthy relationships.

A good example is my sister. We would clash a lot over cultural and faith issues. Ironically enough, I wasn't so much upset with her views. When she disagreed with me, I saw it as a sign of disrespect. As 15 years her senior, I expected her to listen to me, just as I listened to my grandfather.

In other words, what upset me was a realization that what helped me cope with my abusive grandfather was not going to work in adult life. The way my family communicated discontent was either by yelling (confrontation) or avoiding (dodging). Because I hated screaming, I'd distance myself, hoping that my sister would notice and make appropriate amends.

Then one day, our conversations turned upside down. I don't know what prompted this change, so my best guess is that the Holy Spirit intervened.

Instead of me talking and expecting her to listen, I listened and allowed her to talk. I gave her time without any expectations. Our conversation drifted towards our dreams and more specifically, our shared passion for writing as well as for reading great writers. I became so comfortable with her that I shared my fear of being too old to quit Exxon and start a new career.

She responded by sharing how she bumped into some sixty-year-old hippie-looking guy who introduced himself to her as *"an activist."* In the past, I'd dismiss that type of person as a loser, but now I was laughing my butt off.

The kind of laughter that drowned out fear and made me see my sister in a whole new light: <u>a dear friend</u>. Instead of expecting respect, I got something better, someone who believes in me. I couldn't help but reciprocate. As such, our relationship continues to get better and better.

One day I was brainstorming on how to set productive ground rules for a facilitation gig. The company that hired me wanted me to break through silos, and I figured that the best way to open them up is to share a couple of simple stories.

I found a story about a lady who decided to pray until an angel showed up and answered her intention. She blocked everything and everyone out so that she wouldn't get distracted. Even when someone was tapping on her shoulder, she ignored it, because she was on the mission to pray until an angel showed up. As it turns out, the person tapping on her shoulder was the angel with the answer to her prayers, but because he couldn't get her attention, he moved on.

Isn't it similar to us? Don't we get so caught up on what we expect to see that we miss the answers to our prayers?

In the case of my sister, I expected her respect for the time I was spending on her, and it was a train wreck. When I gave her time without any expectations, I got something even better: an ally who still encourages me to keep going when the going gets tough.

Establishing a healthy relationship with my sister was an excellent warm-up for my romantic partnership with Jessi. I realized that the Control Driven part of me wanted a woman to praise me because I wanted evidence that I was investing my time in the right person. <u>I wanted a wife for what she did for me, not for who she was</u>. That's not sustainable nor enjoyable.

As a Love Driven Man, I decided NOT to look for a woman whose praise for me came from flattery. I wanted a spouse I could love for who she is, rather than what she did. I didn't even think about or look for evidence that a particular person was an answer to my prayers. I just wanted to be with her. I wanted our time together to transcend all expectations.

In the case of my sister, I was blessed to see the immediate benefits of giving time without expectations. However, just like when it came to my wife search, you will come across times when in spite of your best, selfless intentions, you'll feel like a failure. You'll feel like you have a heart of a champion, but no medal to show for it.

To persevere, you'll need tremendous patience. The kind that only comes from God.

How to take steps of faith #2:
Relying on God for results

When we are generous without any particular expectations, our mind becomes vulnerable to doubt. The suspicion that what we are doing isn't God's work tends to grow stronger the longer we don't see tangible results. It's not so much about being selfish, but wondering whether our time could make more of an impact if we were to spend it somewhere else.

The experience that clinched it for me came when I was a Life Teen Core member. Life Teen is an organization that aims to bring teens closer to Christ.

> The main idea behind Life Teen is to bring in High School students after Sunday's mass to learn more about their faith by meeting them where they are. We would warm up through group games, music, and a lot of laughs. Then one of the youth ministers would speak. They did not shy away from tough topics. For example, we discussed pornography, sex, and suicide. I learned a ton myself! For the remainder of the time, we would break into small groups to share our reactions to the material. That's where my partner Jeanne and I would come in. The first year I did it, our group averaged four people, so it was easy to stay focused and

develop a connection. It was a great way to start my Life Teen Core member experience.

With that positive experience in mind, I went into the following year, feeling pretty good about myself. This time around, however, my group averaged 14 people, and keeping everyone focused seemed like mission impossible. I would ask a question, then say, *"Put that phone down, John."* Someone would be sharing, and I would have to break my focus to say, *"James, please sit down!"* Or I'd be saying something and would have to turn to a side conversation and say, *"Can I have your attention, please,"* because I was losing my train of thought!

I felt crushed because I didn't feel like I was making a difference. Yes, there would be moments when everyone was paying attention and listening, but they were very few and far between. I felt like I was doing something wrong or maybe that I was not good enough to do this in the first place. I felt out of options, so I turned to God!

The Control Driven part of me wanted a clear return on my investment as evidence that I was spending my time wisely. For example, a group session where all of the teens were super engaged and gave clear indications of how their faith life exploded as a result of our time together! That's what I expected — a clear and present validation of my efforts.

I prayed for these kinds of results, but that's not what I was getting. Instead, I got something better. A sense of peace that came through understanding that **when it comes to serving God, the perfect is always the enemy of good.**

I remembered what one of the youth ministers said during our orientation meetings. "Your job is to plant the seeds and let the Holy Spirit do the work. Whenever you get too wrapped up in the results, you are making it about yourself."

I realized that I was "planting seeds" all right, but my expectations of immediate results distracted me from why I was there in the first place — being an instrument of God's plan.

God knows we are imperfect creatures who crave signs that keep us headed in the right direction. So I got mine at Life Teen as well.

> It was the last meeting of the year, right before Christmas. I asked who would want to close our session with a prayer. To my surprise, one of the most distracting boys volunteered. I closed my eyes and braced myself for impact. I thought to myself, *"Please don't be too judgmental!"*
>
> He started praying. Wow, it was so profound and insightful! This guy was pouring his heart out to God. I was stunned.

In that instant, I got a massive lesson in relying on God for results. The thing is that this young man was still distracting the following semester – this was no instant conversion for sure. It didn't matter though. His prayer showed me that even though my efforts seemed hopeless, God works in all of us, all the time. Results will come. They will be bigger than my mind can imagine. I felt blessed for the privilege of experiencing just a small sample.

When we rely solely on our efforts for results, our Control Driven side will look for superficial evidence. If we don't see proof soon enough, we'll be tempted to quit as I was with Life Teen. Consequently, as a Love Driven Man, I removed myself from situations where I squeezed out God, where I was tempted to give the appearances the final say.

My desire to rely on God for results led me to delete my online dating profiles. I am not criticizing dating apps in general. In my case, I noticed how "shopping" the profiles of women conditioned me to think that I could backward engineer an ideal match from things that are really just superficial, things like photos, education, career, and even height. As a 6'4" man, I didn't want my woman to be too short! I'd paint myself an impossible picture of what I wanted the person to be like from an online snapshot and then ignored the red flags because I didn't want to be lonely.

When I got dumped, or I couldn't ignore the reality anymore, and I dumped the other person, I would go back to the ever-fresh supply of new profiles. New fantasies, I was fooling myself by thinking that if I persisted and threw enough things on the wall, eventually something would stick. I looked for perfect, and that's why I missed the good.

After five years of the online dating madness, I decided that it was time to get off the hamster wheel and rely on God for results.

My mind had no idea how this could work out, and that was precisely the point. I finally gave God space to work in what I considered most precious area of my life: romantic relationships. It took another year, but the pain and frustration turned into a joyful testimony when I met my wife, Jessi, at a Catholic retreat!

Conclusion

My official introduction to Tyler Perry came from watching *Boo 2! A Madea Halloween*, with Jessi. I didn't get it. Here was a big guy dressed up as an older woman clowning around with some other crazy characters. Total silliness that made Jessi, my fiancée at the time, laugh super hard. And because she was laughing, I couldn't help but chuckle myself.

As it turns out, Tyler Perry has a lot more depth to him than what appears in the *Madea* movies. About a year later, I attended a *Live2Lead* event[8] where I heard Tyler say, *"Don't despise small beginnings."*

He felt frustrated for many years because nobody was noticing nor valuing his work. Tyler had to endure the many times when only a few people showed up for his events. He found himself manning the concession stand during intermission at his shows or even sleeping in the car to make ends meet. It would have been easy for him to despise the lack of progress and quit. But he didn't quit – he kept going, and now he owns one of the largest studios in the United States that employs 30,000 people.

Looking back, Tyler credits the humble beginnings for teaching him to give time to his vision without expectations as preparation for massively better opportunities. He learned that not every opportunity was for him, which allowed him to rely on God for results. His faith grew. That was the best result.

Whenever your mind sees nothing but bad news and your desire to control pulls you towards surrender, don't be like General Hull and give up. It's time to start taking steps of faith and give God control.

THE LOVE DRIVEN MAN

According to Tyler Perry, "It's okay to start small as long as you start. A lot of times, it's better that way."[9]

Take baby steps towards giving your time without expectation and relying on God for results. The more you do that, the more natural Proverbs 3:5 way of life will become. You'll grow as a Love Driven Man!

You'll follow what matters eternally even while surrounded by the seemingly insurmountable odds.

Chapter 5 Reflection Questions:

What life problems seem insolvable to your mind?

Are they genuinely unsolvable, or is your mind just stuck in the past?

Is your mind clinging to God or to the past hurts?

How can you give more time without expectations?

How can you rely more on God for results?

Chapter 6: Keeping God #1
Am I trying to become a god,
or is God #1 in my life?

"What profit is the idol when its maker has carved it, Or an image, a teacher of falsehood? For its maker trusts in his own handiwork when he fashions speechless idols."
Habakkuk 2:18 (NASB)

A Control Driven Man idolizes capabilities, which results in him trying to become a god.

A Love Driven Man focuses on allowing God to lead in his life to make sure that God is # 1.

In this chapter, I'll explain the two most effective ways of allowing God to lead – preventing tactics from running your strategy and restarting with God.

I grew up thinking that Frankenstein was an old school attempt at horror movies. I saw a big guy in a black and white film with some silly looking screws sticking out of his neck, and I wasn't scared. Maybe that's what did the trick decades ago, but in the age of Stephen King and CGI, I was yawning. The significance of the story didn't hit me until years later. I listened to a lecture on a CD as I commuted to work when I heard the following quote from the book: "You are my creator, but I am your master; - obey!"[10]

Meaning, the main character's seemingly noble plans resulted in a monster that ended up controlling him.

This quote hit me hard because it was a perfect analogy for my well-intentioned efforts to create panaceas that resulted in monsters. I was so focused on learning the right tools that I didn't realize I was becoming a god ruled by my own creation. For I created a mindset that was supposed to attract solutions into my life, but instead it hijacked my life and got between me and God.

In my mid-thirties I was so unhappy with my life, that I was open to anything. I thought nothing had worked for me to date! My desire to get control back of my life back led me to New Age ideas. I tried many of them, and at first, they gave me a lot of excitement. I felt like I finally got the insider's guide to life. I thought, *"Now I know how celebrities do it!"*

The one idea in particular that had me excited was that *"Everything is an illusion."*

"Yes! That's how successful people become successful," I thought. *"They understand that this world is moldable, and with that knowledge they can 'manifest' their desires into being."*

Oh yes, I tried *"manifesting."* For example, before going to bed, I used to imagine myself being on the Oprah Winfrey show. I don't know what I was on that show for or what my message was - I was going to let the *"universe"* decide.

But the more I did that, the more unsettled I became. I realized that the *"manifesting"* I did was all about me, and it made God unnecessary.

The first time that I realized something was wrong, was when I couldn't figure out how my visit to Oprah was going to further the kingdom of God. This realization made me feel selfish.

The straw that broke the camel's back was remembering Jesus in the garden of Gethsemane, sweating blood as he was praying to the Father to take away his imminent crucifixion. (Luke 22:40-46)

Even though Jesus could eliminate the pain, he didn't. As God, the Son, he chose to obey God, the Father. For if He avoided the cross, thereby denying that He was the Messiah, He would be giving control to the people he had created. Even more importantly, if Jesus were not our sacrifice, no one would be saved. Jesus, the Lamb of God chose to die for us. He embraced Our Father's plan.

"But he was pierced for our transgressions, he was crushed for our iniquities; the punishment that brought us peace was on him, and by his wounds we are healed."
Isaiah 53:5 (NIV)

Consequently, we are all eternally grateful that Jesus didn't treat His mission as an illusion.

Jesus' example showed me that my abilities, no matter how powerful, will always take a backseat to our Heavenly Father. Obedience is difficult for us because the drift of the world is so subtle that we don't even notice when we end up replacing God with our own tactics. We think we are creating love, but we end up manipulated by our good intentions.

How to allow God to lead #1:

Preventing tactics from running your strategy

I learned the difference between tactics and strategies at West Point.

"Tactics" are how units fight on the ground. For example, when I was in Ranger school, I learned the various battle drills such as react to contact or platoon attack.

The "strategy," on the other hand, is the Generals' plan to win the war.

For example, the First Gulf War was as flawless as it gets because the tactics and strategy were planned and carried out correctly. The Second Gulf War was also great as long as we fought the regular Iraqi army of soldiers in uniforms. Once the war turned into an insurgency, our strategy did not adjust fast enough to fight the enemy who didn't soldier conventionally. The conflict turned into a quagmire until General Petraeus came with a new and significantly more effective strategy, which in turn made our tactics productive again.

I always had an affinity for exploring life's tactics and strategies. Even as a Computer Science major at West Point, I eagerly read the books for my philosophy class. Many cadets rolled their eyes, but I was in heaven! During combat deployments or my time on construction vessels in West Africa, I kept searching for meaning through books like *Brothers Karamazov* or *The Purpose Driven Life*. In later years, as I began to realize that I'd never be happy in a corporate job, my search for an alternate career led me to become a life coach.

"If I so enjoy getting the most out of life, wouldn't it be cool if I got to do it for a living?" was the question I pondered.

Consequently, I decided to do an eight-month training program to become a certified life coach, which included three in-person training sessions in Austin. It wasn't so much that I wanted to do it. I was just so desperate to be passionate about my career. Given my self-help topic interests, it seemed like a pretty good educated guess. I asked myself, *"Why not?"* So, I signed up.

THE LOVE DRIVEN MAN

When I showed up on a Friday morning to the first in-person training session, I heard music and saw people dancing. I said to myself: *"Oh my goodness, I made a huge mistake!"*

Back then, I was still very much a people-pleaser, so I thought it would be rude to leave. Also, I had paid a lot of money to take this course, so, I stayed!

The training blew me away. The instructor was a British woman who was molested by her older brother growing up, and she explained how a new belief system helped her build a happy life. In the process, I saw everyone responding, opening up, and just being so accepting. I had never before experienced anything like that.

Although the instructor never called the belief system *"New Age"* ideas, I'll use this terminology as a label. A quick google search defines New Age as *"a broad movement characterized by alternative approaches to traditional Western culture."* [11] That definition is open enough to encompass my experiences as well as many other teachings you are likely coming across in your life right now.

New Age ideas provide great alternatives when problem-solving, but cause trouble when they become a foundation for your life. A lot of the New Age concepts have the tactics right, but because they ignore God, the strategy fails in the long run. It's similar to Vietnam, where the US won every single battle yet lost the war. The tactics were excellent – almost too good, because the tactical superiority distracted the US leadership from the fact that the overall plan was terrible. <u>Just like you cannot win a war without a good strategy, you cannot find eternal life without God.</u>

A good example is a typical New Age principle that *"Everything is Energy."*[12] This law encourages choices that attract *"good energy."* The theory champions *"win/win scenarios"* and it discourages *"bad energy"* choices like feeling sad. The *"energetic"* way of thinking was very intriguing to me at first, because I wanted what it promised! I wanted to have the energy that comes with feeling passionate about something. Aren't passionate people super energetic? I experienced a lot of *"bad energy"* that my coaching certification called *"level 1."* You experience this level when you feel like you always lose or when you are basically feeling down.

At the tactical level, you don't want to look depressed because other people will perceive you as weak and avoid you. As an entrepreneur, I learned first-hand the importance of not letting rejecting "No's" get me down. If I lose my energy, potential clients will be less likely to hire me, and I'd risk falling into a downward spiral.

But strategically, if I only go for high-level energy experiences, I deprive myself of an opportunity to grieve and a chance to connect with the Lord. Suffering is redemptive. Just like Jesus chose to suffer to open up Heaven for us, so we also must walk through pain to resurrect something greater. After my former wife left me for her boss at work, I took our divorce very hard. I probably grieved longer than an *"energetic"* leader should. This time was actually extremely well spent, because, in that seemingly extended grieving, I finally connected to the words of scripture that used to go in one ear and go out the other – verses like these:

"Blessed are those who mourn, for they shall be comforted."
Matthew 5:4 (NASB)

"A time to cry and a time to laugh. A time to grieve and a time to dance."
Ecclesiastes 3:4 (NLT)

So yes, by all means, use effective tactics, but don't let them take over the ultimate strategy of getting closer to God.

The Control Driven Man clings to tactics because he can see immediate results. A Love Driven Man understands that following Jesus rarely produces results in the short term. When those results come, however, they are always more impactful than what even the best of tactics could have ever produced. It's hard not to get caught up in tactics, especially when the Control Driven world heavily promotes them. To keep our eyes on God, regularly ask yourself if God is at the core of everything you do.

How to allow God to lead #2:
Restarting with God

We want to know why?

"Why?" is the most-commonly asked question that kids ask.

The only thing that changes in our adulthood is that we don't ask *"Why?"* out loud anymore.

Whenever someone else gets a promotion, or we get sick, or maybe our partner walks out on us we ask, *"Why?"*

So much so, Simon Sinek wrote the best-selling book *Start with Why*[13] to make a point that everything we do must start with a good reason.

Focusing on the *"why"* **alone** speaks to our mind's desire to control, because we do what we think makes sense and we avoid what doesn't. Our souls, however, are not of this world. They are eternal, and whenever we get too caught up on the "why," we forget who we are. Pierre Teilhard de Chardin famously wrote: *"We are NOT human beings having a spiritual experience. We are spiritual beings having a human experience."*[14]

Saint Augustine is my favorite saint. I love him because he is so relatable. For Exhibit A, check out this quote: *"Lord, give me chastity, but do not give it to me just yet."*[15] Augustine was brilliant, and in his early years, continually looked for answers to life's "why" questions.

He would follow various teachings, but eventually, pull away because none of them gave Augustine satisfactory explanations. That all changed at the age of 31 when he heard the voice of a child singing a song: *"Pick it up and read it. Pick it up and read it."* He took the words as a divine command to open the Bible and read the first passage he came to, which was:

"Not in carousing and drunkenness, not in sexual excess and lust, not in quarreling and jealousy. Rather, put on the Lord Jesus Christ, and make no provision for the desires of the flesh."
Romans 13:13-14 (BSB)

Augustine, who always searched for a more in-depth explanation, closed the book.[16] He finally found what he had been looking for all these years. Something far more significant than his mind could have expected. He restarted with God and his heart received an infusion of clarity, which, much like light, vanquished the gloom of doubt.

Many years, down the road, when he wrote his autobiography called *The Confessions of Augustine,* in the first paragraph, he included the following statement: *"You have made us for yourself, O Lord, and our heart is restless until it rests in you."*

We'll never know the answers to every *"why."*

We can't, because this world is not our final destination. Eternity is.

Whenever you get discouraged or bogged down, go back to the basics: God.

Through the scriptures God will speak to your heart and get you moving in the right direction.

As I am writing this chapter, I am experiencing difficulty in ramping up my business. From the corporate measurement perspective, I'm a failure, and I don't understand why this is happening. I took a big step of faith, and my Control Driven Mind is telling me that I look like a fool. When I shared my fears with my wife, she said that she prays the following verse for me from Psalm 25:3, *"No one who hopes in you will ever be put to shame." (NIV)*

Now every time the doubtful thoughts enter my mind, I restart with God through this passage and the *why* or *how* driven fears fade into the background.

Whenever you are facing fears, rise above your mind's desire to control.

Remind yourself who you are and, more importantly, whose you are.

Go to the scriptures, and you will always find words that will give you the love-fueled restart to keep you driving in the eternal direction.

Conclusion

During my coaching certification, I remember one of the ladies saying something to the effect of: "I go to my Church, but only to keep up with my friends and family. It's a social thing! Now, through these principles, I finally know how I can transform my life."

Even though at the time, I was a reasonably good Christian (I went to church every Sunday and prayed every day), I thought to myself, *"Yeah, it gives me no pleasure to say this, but she's right!"*

I had no way of responding to her. The lack of an adequate comeback stuck with me for a few years, until I met another woman who told me how New Age principles turned her life around. But then out of nowhere, she gave me the downside: *"It puts all of the responsibility on me!"*

Wow, it makes perfect sense!

<u>New Age principles make you believe that you are a god</u>.

That's pretty scary. Isn't it? Every time something doesn't go according to your plans, it's all on you! You are not *"tapping into your highest energy vibration," "not manifesting enough"* or not pulling some other divine lever hard enough.

It's all your responsibility, which makes it pretty stressful to stay obedient if you think about it.

That's why everyone, except for two out of twenty in my certification class, went back to their old life in spite of manifesting incredible futures for themselves during our training. I was one of those two. I took the effective tactics from the certification but grounded my coaching practice on Biblical principles. The other person from my certification who quit her job keeps on bouncing from one New Age-based training to the other, because she thinks she is one secret away from finding the answers.

My friends, making God #1, will give you peace.

Control Driven Men get caught up on short term tactics that provide temporary results.

At the surface, **the god-like capabilities appear very appealing, but the stress of the responsibility will wear you out.** You'll become a prisoner of the very mindset you created.

Keep your strategy centered on Jesus. When your mind questions your reasons, restart with God. Go to the Bible, and you will find the strength to keep going.

As a Love Driven Man, you will lean on God as your foundation that will keep you growing towards the eternal.

Chapter 6 Reflection Questions:

Are you seeking satisfaction in something other than God?

Is God #1 in your life, or are the current trends of today dictating your life?

Are you giving God control, or are you trying to become your own god?

How do you make sure that tactics are not running your strategy?

When you experience setbacks, what helps you restart with God?

Chapter 7: Taking Action
Am I telling myself it's too late,
or am I taking action?

"For I know the plans I have for you,' declares the LORD, 'plans to prosper you and not to harm you, plans to give you hope and a future."
Jeremiah 29:11 (NIV)

A Control Driven Man leads his life in a rigid sequence, which results in assuming that *"it's too late for changes."*

A Love Driven Man leads by example to inspire others to action.

In this chapter, I'll explain the two most effective ways of leading by example – bringing a brick, not a cathedral, and doing the death bed test.

I learned about the "OODA Loop" from an ex-Marine pilot about ten years after I separated from the Army. I wish I had heard about it sooner because it's a simple but very instructive framework for decision-making.

The acronym postulates that decision making occurs in a recurring cycle of four steps: **Observe, Orient, Decide,** and **Act**.

Here's the main point – leaders who circle through the four points faster take more action and, as such, win more often!

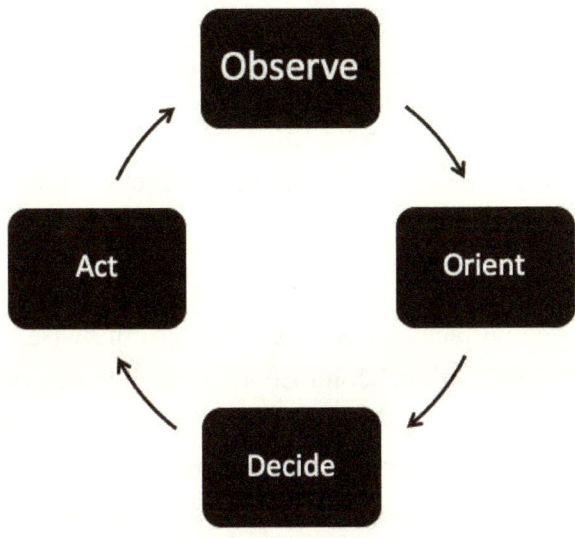

Let me give you a simple business example. Blockbuster used to be the undisputed king of VHS tape rentals. Some of my best high school memories included going to the local Blockbuster to pick up a movie for the night. The store had cool posters and a vast selection. To this day I remember the excitement when the movie that just came out was actually in stock. We weren't a wealthy family, so this was a big deal! But Blockbuster became too comfortable, and its mangers slowed down their OODA loop. They assumed that they were invulnerable.

Along came a hungry startup named Netflix, which OBSERVED an opportunity to ship videos through the post office. VHS tapes were too bulky and fragile to mail, so Netflix DECIDED not to ACT. But when DVDs came out, Netflix ORIENTED itself as a service that didn't have the annoying late return fees. They DECIDED to take on the $16 billion rental industry. Netflix won, but more remarkably, they didn't stop OODA looping. They OBSERVED and quickly

ACTED on streaming and later on content production, which fueled Netflix's growth to $124 billion market value.

On the flip side, Blockbuster didn't ACT to change its business model. As a result, only one location is still open today, down from 9,000 at its peak!

Therefore, the OODA approach favors agility over raw power whenever people face competition, war, or otherwise. The founder of this principle, Colonel John Boyd, applied the theory in the US Air Force, by advocating for less heavily armed, but more maneuverable fighter aircraft. A bold move because in the 1960s, powerful jets like the F-4 Phantom II were the weapon of choice. The power, however, came at the price of agility. The F-4 was so bulky a pilot friend of mine joked that the aircraft was *"a proof that even a brick can fly!"*

Boyd inspired the Lightweight Fighter program (LWF) which produced the successful F-16 and F/A-18 aircraft that are still in use today by the United States and many other allied nations!

I used to feel like a powerful jet, but built for a mission I didn't want to perform anymore. So much so, I remember sitting on a therapist's couch, saying, *"If I could figure out what my passion is, I'd go for it in a heartbeat!"*

Well, I found that passion when I coached. I loved being the miracle that I wish I had experienced when I was younger. I wanted to be someone who shows a new way when a person's mind says, *"There is no way."*

But then the doubts crept in. *"It's too late! Who do you think you are? You're not one of those guys who started a lemonade stand as a kid. You were a fat kid who preferred to play video games! You are getting paid way more than you are worth at ExxonMobil. You'd be a fool to leave."*

In other words, I thought of myself as a heavily equipped jet that was incapable of making extreme life maneuvers.

I prayed and used my training in coaching to work through my fears and at a retreat, I finally decided to cast my doubts aside and go for it. I felt set and ready to go.

Except at that very same retreat, I met Jessi.

Yeah, she was a great woman, but I had thought the same things about other girls. *"It's too late. I can't start a business **and** date."* I was so close to giving up on Jessi, because starting a business by itself was plenty "Mission Impossible" for me already! There was no need to make the insurmountable odds any harder!

I was worried that I'd experience my typical relationship disappointment. Even if, for some strange reason, she did say "Yes" to a date, an attorney like her would never want to marry a dreamer like me. She surely must be looking for someone who is a real provider – a provider with a high, steady income. Someone who works for a company like Exxon.

I was worried about falling in love with Jessi because it would mean giving up the coaching dream that God placed in my heart.

I felt it was just too late to do both.

As a Control Driven Man, I was wary of too much change. I was okay with some course adjustments here and there, but F-16 type life maneuvers were completely outside of my comfort zone. When it came to pursuing the dreams that God placed in my heart, I wanted to be a Love Driven Man who led by example. But my mind told me to be careful. *"It's too late for drastic changes!"*

Whenever our mind gets worried about our life getting too much out of sequence, **we have to remind ourselves that when it comes to a God-inspired calling, we don't need to have everything figured out. We just need to take the next step!**

How to lead with action #1:
Bringing a brick, not a cathedral

When I think of leadership, the first image that comes to my mind is someone giving an inspiring speech. In the movies you often see the hero give such a speech before an impossible feat. I'm thinking here *"The Game of Inches"* from Oliver Stone's *Any Given Sunday* or *Henry V*'s *"St Crispin's Day."* Never mind that these came from multimillion-dollar films or one of the greatest writers in the English language. That was my gold standard!

Since speeches like that didn't pop out of me at a snap of a finger, I figured that the next best thing I could do is prepare and over-prepare I did! Perhaps it's the computer science major in me, but much like a piece of software code, I thought that given enough time, I could turn myself into a universal speaking machine. As well-intentioned as this effort was, among many other things, I found myself so focused on what would make me sound smart that I missed out on what my audience wanted. That's kind of an important thing for a speaker when you intend to create a genuine connection!

As I dug deeper, I realized that whenever I acted at my best, it was always on the spur of the moment — never thinking or planning, just being. I felt like I was handing the reigns over from my brain to my heart. These types of experiences were rare, but they were always unforgettable. In this realm concepts like a carefully sequenced agenda don't exist. I wanted to go to that place more often!

I got a perfect opportunity to practice when the most significant frontier of my fears showed up in my email: an invite to an Improv Meet Up. In an instant, I knew I had to give it a try!

Initially, I did great. I was volunteering, jumping in, and so proud of myself!

However, in our second meeting, when we graduated from warm-up exercises to scenes, my logical brain came back with a vengeance. I froze. I jumped into a scene but couldn't think of anything to say, so I stepped aside and stayed on the sidelines for the rest of the Meet Up feeling bad about myself. I flopped, because I was trying to come up with something fully baked, ideally perfect, and modular.

In other words, I wanted to be in full control instead of following the fundamental rule of improv – "<u>Bring a brick, not a cathedral</u>." I should have contributed something small (a brick) like a word, gesture or a sound, but instead I collapsed under my (cathedral-sized) expectations of having everything fully thought out. I felt so embarrassed because everyone else was just having a good time, and I felt like I made a fool out of myself. The perfectionist in me thought my improv adventure was over. I gave it my best shot, but it just wasn't for me.

Ironically, a weakness sometimes can also very much work in your favor. Just as my bruised ego wanted me to quit, it also didn't want me to admit to my co-workers and friends that I did so. You see, after the first Meet Up, I talked a big game to everyone and their mother about my recent improv adventure; I was literally between a rock and a hard place!

Luckily, both of the organizers reached out to me with words of encouragement, which broke through my *"Catch -22"* stalemate.

I recalled from a creativity class I had taken at the Jung Center that whenever you are stuck, lower the bar. That's what I did when I came back. I reframed my success to be defined by my participation alone; anything more than that would be pure icing on the cake. I am by no means ready to join an improv troop, but where I am now is way farther than I ever imagined. Most importantly, I still prepare for speeches, but when I practice, I permit myself to deviate from the script. I am not quite at the movie level, but I am tremendously proud of my progress!

Further, the improv experience helped me to give Jessi AND entrepreneurship a try.

The Control Driven Man inside of me got scared because I thought I had to have the blueprint figured out before laying the first brick.

The Love Driven Man is far more concerned about where he's putting his trust.

In my case, I knew that the only reason I'd give up starting a relationship AND business was because I didn't trust God. To bring my mind sufficiently on board, I performed the death bed test.

How to lead with action #2:
Doing the death bed test

Reading Leo Tolstoy's *The Death of Ivan Ilych* caused me to spend some quality time reflecting on my own death.[17] In this story, Tolstoy writes about a middle-aged, mid-level government official who one day falls when decorating his large house. The resulting injury marks the beginning of an inescapable end. With each day, Ivan's condition worsens and that pushes him to reflect on his life. He realizes that even though he did what others expected him to do, none of his accomplishments mattered because his life lacked a deeper meaning. Focusing on the work and gaining social status atrophied his ability to love. Only in his last few minutes, right before he dies, does Ivan finally have a moment of empathetic connection with his son.

Even though Tolstoy wrote the book in czarist Russia more than one hundred years ago, his main character struggled with the very same choices I face now.

It's not just me, though. Bronnie Ware is an Australian nurse who spent several years caring for patients in the last weeks of their lives. The insights from her conversations led her to write a book called *The Top Five Regrets of the Dying*. Guess what the top one was? It was: *"I wish I'd dared to live a life true to myself, not the life others expected of me."*[18]

More broadly, all of the regrets boil down to the fact that <u>none of the people regretted what they had done, but rather they regretted what they had not done</u>. **It wasn't a mistake of the wrong action. It was a mistake of putting off taking action.**

THE LOVE DRIVEN MAN

Both the anguish of the fictional character from Tolstoy's book and the disappointments of people on their death bed made me wonder if I am taking enough action to avoid a similar fate.

The OODA loop can help you here, as well. The model explains how we make decisions based on how we perceive the benefits of taking action.

Before making a DECISION to take ACTION, a man will first evaluate whether he can ORIENT himself to take advantage of the information he OBSERVED. Therefore, we can alter the utility we seek at the DECIDE phase by changing how we perceive the information we get at the OBSERVE stage. To put it in even simpler terms, the more we see the glass as half full, the more likely we'll take action. The more we take action, the more often we'll succeed!

Whenever we look at life decisions, it's easy to get caught up in taking the next logical step. Our Control Driven mind feels very comfortable with that, but the more we do it, the more we do what we are expected to do. Unfortunately, the expectations of this world are typically different from what God calls us to do.

That's why a Love Driven Man looks at his choices from the standpoint of his deathbed. **Will the choices I'm making today make me feel fulfilled if I were to die tomorrow?**

That's why I decided to give my business and Jessi a chance. Even if I became the wealthiest man on the planet, then I'd still feel like a failure on my death bed because I would have always wondered if I missed out on true love. As a Love Driven Man, I couldn't let that happen, so I decided to date Jessi. It was the best decision ever, because even now, as a business owner, I feel like she believes in me more than I believe in myself!

Conclusion

As kids, we had an exemplary ability to find alternatives, and we couldn't care less about rigid sequences.

> Whenever my baby brother wasn't happy with the rules, he told his dad, *"You're fired!"* The first time he did that, my mom, stepdad, and I looked at each other with a puzzled look on our faces. Where did he get that? He was only a few years old, and it was almost a decade before *"The Apprentice"* show made the *"You're fired!"* phrase famous.

As we age, we tend to look for the most common answer, and it becomes harder for us to think outside the box. In *A Whack on the Side of the Head,* Roger von Oech[19] tells the story of how his high school sophomore teacher put a small chalk circle on the blackboard. When the teacher asked the class what he just drew, he only got one answer: "A chalk circle on a blackboard." That's it! No one said anything else because the class felt that they gave their teacher "the right" answer.

The teacher responded: "I'm surprised at you. I did the same exercise with a group of kindergartners yesterday, and they thought of 50 things the chalk mark could be: an owl's eye, a cigarette butt, the top of a telephone pole, a pebble, a squashed bug, and so on."[20]

The older we get, the harder it becomes for us to imagine different possibilities.

A Control Driven Man expects to have all the answers before he starts, and because he has a hard time seeing new opportunities, he rarely gets started. After delaying long enough, he feels like it's too late to change.

THE LOVE DRIVEN MAN

A Love Driven Man, on the other hand, knows that the Lord's plans don't lead to harm, so he doesn't let the lack of 100% certainty get in his way. He makes dreams a reality, one brick at a time. A Love Driven Man doesn't wait until everything is in place to build a cathedral. When the going gets tough, the Love Driven Man looks at his choices as if he were lying on his deathbed.

When we look at our life as if we had no time left on this Earth, our heart comes to the forefront and draws us to what matters eternally.

Chapter 7 Reflection Questions:

When do you tell yourself it's too late?

What prevents you from taking a step of faith?

Are you listening to God or your past?

What helps you bring a brick, not a cathedral?

How often do you do the death bed test?

Chapter 8: Progress Measurement
Am I focusing on the right type of progress?

"We also rejoice in our sufferings, because we know that suffering produces perseverance; perseverance, character; and character, hope. And hope does not disappoint us."
Romans 5:3-5 (BSB)

A Control Driven Man looks for physical progress, which brings temporary happiness.

A Love Driven Man looks for emotional growth that brings sustainable joy.

In this chapter, I'll explain the two most effective ways of ensuring that your heart is opening up to what matters eternally - laughing at setbacks and finding a deeper purpose behind slow progress.

I grew up with Aesop's fables. I'd watch them even in communist Poland, but until now, I thought that they were ancient Chinese stories. As it turns out, Aesop was a slave, and a storyteller believed to have lived in Ancient Greece. One of the stories that stuck in my mind is about a goose who laid a golden egg every day. Upon discovery, the owner started selling the eggs and began to grow in wealth. After a while, however, he became impatient with the daily interval and got an idea that he could get all of the eggs instantly if he just cut open the goose. He killed her but found no gold. Even worse, the daily eggs stopped! The ending of the story provides a very instructive moral, which is just as accurate today as it was over 2,500 years ago when Aesop wrote the story: *"Those who have plenty want more and so lose all they have."*

In the Army, no amount of recognition was enough for me. When I first started West Point, I didn't even know if I could make it past basic training. However, when I graduated in the top 10% of my class, I wished I had tried harder and graduated in the top 5% so that I could have earned an honor grad title! My desire for recognition intensified on active duty. I first focused on getting a Ranger tab and later various combat badges.

All of this led me to ExxonMobil, where I signed on for the big paycheck and benefits. As a Control Driven Man, I went for the tangible metrics like badges and bank account balances. I ended up miserable because I thought that happiness would follow these achievements, but that never materialized. Yes, I got temporary happiness boosts, but those wore off very quickly. Much like the farmer with the golden egg laying goose, I made some stupid decisions, because I was too obsessed with accelerating my golden egg production.

The Control Driven side of me didn't disappear, even when I quit my corporate career to pursue full-time coaching. When I got my first client, I was happy, but shortly after, I wanted a second. The first time I had two clients at the same time, I was excited, but when I went down to one instead of three or more, I became disappointed.

The Love Driven Man in me was grateful that I could make money doing something I love, but the Control Driven part started pressuring me to show constant growth. The desire to control is innate and will surface whenever our influence appears to be shrinking. How you handle these inevitable perceptions will demonstrate how much you've grown as a Love Driven Man.

THE LOVE DRIVEN MAN

How do you know this Love Driven thing is working? #1:
Laughing at setbacks

I periodically co-host a podcast named *"Heart for Excellence,"* where I have an opportunity to hear the testimonies of mostly men, but also women, who have made a ton of mistakes. The guests openly lay out their messy pasts, and it's some painful stuff. The kind of setbacks that most keep hidden as their darkest secrets. Our guests, however, laugh them off.

I came to this realization when one of the guys we interviewed started chuckling as he was telling us his *"brilliant"* idea of opening a gun store. Even though this venture ended in bankruptcy and put a massive strain on his family, he made proper amends and grew from the experience. I knew he meant what he said through his laughter.

I also knew it because I used to be deeply ashamed of my divorce. I kept it as a dark secret because I thought that anyone who found out would consider me to be defective. After a great deal of reflection and internal change, I am finally in a position to freely laugh at how uninformed and unexperienced I was in my first marriage.

But it took me about seven years to get there. In the meantime, I kept beating myself up over the seemingly inexistent physical progress - a divorced guy who couldn't stay in a relationship for more than a few months. Yes, that's a long time, but interestingly enough, I was doing a lot better than I thought. That's because as time went on, I began to laugh at my romantic setbacks!

Laughing might sound like a silly thing, but it's an outward indicator that failure is losing its grip on us, and we are ready to move forward.

Unfortunately, I resisted embracing humor because I felt like frustration and hiding my feelings were more productive. Both, however, got in the way of making genuine connections with people. Frustration put a lot of pressure on me to make relationships work, in spite of the red flags. Hiding my true feelings, on the other hand, blocked the vulnerability required to build a solid foundation for lasting relationships. That's why in Proverbs 17:22 we read, *"A cheerful heart is good medicine, but a broken spirit saps a person's strength." (NLT)*

So, when you find yourself laughing at yourself after failure, embrace it.

Laughter is a greater sign of progress than physical accomplishments because such things come and go. What remains is the ability to find joy in every circumstance.

A Control Driven Man gets caught up in keeping score, and it's only a matter of time until tangible progress leads to disappointment. The real problem is not in keeping score but in the disappointments. Disappointment leads to frustration and the more frustrated we become, the less likely we are to keep going.

By laughing off his setbacks, a Love Driven Man stops wasting precious time dealing with hopelessness and focuses on what matters most — taking action.

Just the other day, I checked my YouTube channel, and I noticed a couple of views. Even though it was a small number, it was better than nothing, so I got excited. I started picturing the beginning of my YouTube mega-stardom, when all of a sudden, I noticed a thumbs down on one of my videos. My first thumbs down! Instantly I felt my heart thumping like I did when I was facing criticism from my grandfather all those years ago. Fortunately, that lasted all of a few seconds, before I broke out in laughter.

My Control Driven old-self would have probably felt down for the rest of the day and quite possibly quit video making altogether.

As a Love Driven Man, the experience reminded me of a very successful social media influencer, Gary Vee, who said how, in the beginning, he got comments like *"Shut the f*ck up wine boy!"*[21]

I laughed as I thought to myself that I might be finally on a celebrity track after all because I got some negative feedback. Whether or not it's true, doesn't matter. What matters is that I didn't waste time feeling depressed over the negative feedback. I got pumped up about my attitude and that kept me focused on what matters most, staying obedient to God's calling. So I continue to make videos regardless of the receptions they get. I know that with time, I will get better. I am full of hope!

Laughing at the setbacks is a great progress indicator because it shows that you can deal with failures productively. However, when you look at the future and feel discouraged, you will feel better when you search for God amidst the frustrations.

How do you know this Love Driven thing is working? #2:

Finding a deeper purpose behind the slow progress.

Whenever I take a step of faith, and it doesn't look like I am progressing, no matter how much I laugh at my setbacks, it feels very discouraging. I am tempted to think that my faith had given me nothing more but unnecessary suffering.

Why take a step forward if it's going to result in two steps back?

In such times, I can't help but think of Job. Job was God's exemplary servant who lost his children, his wealth, and as if that wasn't enough, became covered in excruciating boils. His friends thought that the best way to help him was to get Job to admit that he must have done something to provoke his misfortune. Now keep in mind that Job is the oldest book in the Bible, believed by scholars to be written over 4 thousand years ago. Yet, even then, people had the karma-like perception that if you are experiencing hardship, then you must have done something wrong. You are merely hiding it, or you haven't figured it out yet.

Job does get his answer, but it's nothing like our Control Driven Minds would expect. God shows up. In a beautiful, long monologue, God essentially says, *"Job, how can I possibly explain to you something that you cannot understand?"* (Job chapters 38-41). To a reader, it seems like a non-answer, but to Job, it's plenty, because he encountered God. Job repented, and God gave him twice what he had before. (Job 42)

The Control Driven Man in me is tempted to interpret the suffering that comes from slow progress as a test. Once I eventually pass, God will show up and pay me back double. However, I see the potential for a more in-depth explanation.

When we wait, and it feels like it's been too long, it's time to stop looking for reasons and just start looking for God.

The Love Driven Man understands that much like Job, he will never know the answers, but when he finds God, the suffering will have meaning. The reward may not always be monetary but will always come with something even better, a deeper appreciation of life's mysteries and a closer union with God.

I experienced a lot of ups and down in my entrepreneurial journey. The highs are high, but lows always seem too plentiful. Initially, I thought the feeling of defeat is mostly proving grounds for the new arrivals - a boot camp of sorts, but then I heard a speech by a successful entrepreneur Rachel Hollis who said: *"A Leader never has two good days in a row."*[22]

Hearing those words was a relief! Being a leader is demanding, and in fact, I know that I'm leading precisely because I'm facing a lot of difficulties. But I don't want to stop there because I *get* to encounter God in my frustrations. For example, I have a super supportive wife. Perhaps I wouldn't appreciate her nearly as much if I had become successful more quickly. Jessi always offers me prayers and the right Scriptures. And it doesn't just stop there. I've met a ton of great people who I wouldn't even have bothered to talk to had I become an overnight sensation, because I would have considered them *"small potatoes."*

Hard times are an infallible filter because you quickly find out who is there for you, not the perks. Oh, and don't forget the stories! If things would have always worked out for me, what would I have put in this book? I'd have no lessons learned that I could share! In short, hardships give me an opportunity to appreciate my blessings and to see God in a way that instant prosperity never could!

No one I know enjoys suffering, but every great person I came across found meaning in the wait. They are the people who not only possess transformational knowledge but, even more importantly, have the empathy to convey it in a way that you can't help but listen.

Conclusion

Michael Jordan is the greatest basketball player of his generation, quite possibly of all the time. Even though I had never watched an NBA game, I knew who he was. As a Control Driven Man, I assumed that he was a born natural, who was lucky to win the basketball gene lottery. I'll never forget seeing a commercial that challenged my success beliefs for the first time. On TV I saw footage of Michael making all sorts of mistakes as his voice narrated the following:

"I've missed more than 9000 shots in my career. I've lost almost 300 games. 26 times I've been trusted to take the game-winning shot and missed. I've failed over and over and over again in my life. And that is why I succeed."[23]

The point is perspective.

We don't have enough time, access, or even attention to learn the celebrity's entire story. We only see the wins, because the moment an athlete or a leader stops winning, he or she quickly fades into obscurity. We hear about failures only if they are part of a comeback story and only to serve as a highlight that makes success appear even more successful.

Yes, of course, I'm sure Jordan's genetics played a part, but didn't God give us ALL a soul that allows us to be elite spiritual athletes?

A Control Driven Man wastes time wrapped up in his physical progress, something that never satisfies in the long term, causes us to lose hope, and eventually results in stupid decisions.

THE LOVE DRIVEN MAN

A Love Driven Man finds humor in his setbacks. Not that he is delusional, but because he understands the temptations that come with taking ourselves too seriously in our temporary, earthly home.

And when the progress seems slow, a Love Driven Man looks for God, because in God, he finds an eternal perspective that transforms his grief into a deeper meaning.

The deeper meaning, in turn, becomes a greater appreciation of what is everlasting – union with God.

Chapter 8 Reflection Questions:

How do you measure your life's progress?

Does your way of measuring life's progress bring you joy?

How do you know your heart is opening up to what matters eternally?

How often do you laugh at your setbacks?

What helps you find a deeper purpose behind slow progress?

Parting Words

"What, then, shall we say in response to these things? If God is for us, who can be against us?"
Romans 8:31 (NIV)

When I think of an elephant waiting in a circus tent, I typically recall a chain staked into the ground. Until recently, I just accepted this without much thought. But then I watched a video by my high school friend, Dhar Mann, which made me question how such a small stake can restrain a huge elephant. As it turns out, the shallowly grounded chain is enough, because it used to be enough when the elephant was a baby. The young elephant tried to rip it out, but he wasn't strong enough then, so he continues to assume that he won't be strong enough now, in spite of gaining hundreds of pounds.

Similarly, our mind can become tied down by a chain that we don't think we can rip out. The chain comes out of our failures. There was a time when we weren't strong enough to overcome a particular obstacle, and our mind created a leash to keep us from experiencing pain again. Our life experiences and particularly our mistakes make us stronger. We get better, but just like the elephant, we miss the fact that we can rip out the chain with ease.

I hope that as you read this book, you've realized that you are a lot stronger than you think, and you've identified the mental chains prime for ripping.

Growing in your ability to love is a process.

It's not going to happen overnight, and you'll never reach perfection. The progress will become the reward, as you'll start noticing eternal consequences behind your actions. An average person makes 35,000 decisions in a day. That is 35,000 opportunities to build a stronger relationship with God. What would happen if you made just 10 of those decisions based on what brings more love to your life? And oh, by the way, that's not even a third of 1% of the decisions you make each day!

Bill Gates famously said, "Most people overestimate what they can do in one year and underestimate what they can do in ten years."[24]

Remember that when you judge your progress short term, it will rarely seem to be enough.

Keep at it!

For if you are after making an impact that echoes in eternity, even your Control Driven side, will admit that you are playing a long game.

With God, anything is possible, and typically when going gets tough, that's when you know you are close. To what who knows, but I know that it will exceed your expectations!

Finally, I hope this book doesn't lead you to turn off your mind altogether.

God gave us a brain to keep us safe on Earth. After all, you wouldn't want to live in a world where everyone drove their cars by heart alone!

Instead, I hope that you are better equipped to use your mind as an asset for opening up your heart to what matters eternally.

Our logical side is a great tool, but an uninspiring master.

I want to wrap up with a final transportation analogy.

THE LOVE DRIVEN MAN

The Control Driven Man leads with the mind and hopes his heart will follow.

The Love Driven Man, on the other hand, leads with the heart and uses his mind to help him get there.

God bless you and your journey!

Appendix A: Additional Resources

If you found *The Love Driven Man* useful, then please check out the following resources that will help you build on what you've learned in this book:

1. To share your successes and get encouragement, join "The Love Driven Man Group" on Facebook:
   https://www.facebook.com/groups/TheLoveDrivenManGroup

2. Sign up for a complimentary "Relationship Audit":
   http://www.cs1mindset.com/relationship-audit/

Appendix B: The Love Driven Man Reflection Summary

To receive a free, printable PDF version of this appendix, please visit: http://www.cs1mindset.com/The-Love-Driven-Man/

The online version of Appendix B will also provide you with ideas on how you can form a "Fire Team" to expedite the growth through the power of a small accountability group.

Chapter 1: Your Godly Identity
Am I controlling people's perceptions or uncovering my own godly identity?

"For you did not receive the spirit of slavery to fall back into fear, but you have received the Spirit of adoption as sons, by whom we cry, 'Abba! Father!'"
Romans 8:15

A Control Driven Man wants people to admire him, which results in a need to control his identity to fit other people's expectations.

A Love Driven Man's goal is to cherish his personal identity in Christ, which helps him let go of any desire to control the uncontrollable and instead to grow in love for what matters eternally.

How to uncover your godly identity #1: Growth in the prayer life

How to uncover your godly identity #2: Developing an emotional connection with the Bible

Reflection Questions:

Where does your identity come from?

Do you let others see the real you, or do you carefully control how others see you?

Is your identity coming from God or your wounds?

How can you grow in your prayer life?

How can you build a stronger emotional connection with the Bible?

Chapter 2: Growing Closer to God
Am I seeking validation in accomplishments or in growing closer to God?

"Take delight in the Lord, and he will give you the desires of your heart."
Psalm 37:4 (NIV)

A Control Driven Man wants to earn people's admiration, which results in him having a focus on his accomplishments.

A Love Driven Man's goal is to grow in virtue, which brings him closer to God.

How to grow virtue #1: Removing sin

How to grow virtue #2: Putting yourself on God's timeline

Reflection Questions:

Where does your sense of worth come from?

Does it come from who you are, or what you do?

Is God your master, or are accomplishments your master?

What is your biggest sin? How can you start rooting it out of your life?

Think of a time when God's timing proved to be better than your timetable. How can you see more of God's timing in your life?

Chapter 3: Partnering with Women
Do I use women, or do I partner with women?

"Then the Lord God said, 'It is not good that the man should be alone; I will make him a helper as his partner.'"
Genesis 2:18 (NRSV)

A Control Driven Man wants a woman to make him feel better. He uses her.

A Love Driven Man's goal is to experience love at its fullest. He partners with her.

How to experience love at its fullest #1: Partnering with a woman who will help you follow God's will

How to experience love at its fullest #2: Assuming positive intent

Reflection Questions:

Does your romantic partner (past or present) say things to you that imply she doesn't understand you? How often?

Are you able to be honest with your romantic partner, or are there things that you are hiding (past or present)?

Are you asking God for help, or are you passively waiting for changes in your relationship (past or present)?

What can you change in your relationship so that the two of you help each other get closer to God? If you are single, apply it to your relationship search.

How can you leverage the inevitable conflict to get closer to each other? If you are single, apply it to your relationship search.

Chapter 4: Transforming the Pain
Am I covering up the past
or letting God transform the pain?

"So if anyone is in Christ, there is a new creation: everything old has passed away; see, everything has become new!"
2 Corinthians 5:17 (NRSV)

A Control Driven Man wants to be perfect, which results in covering up the past.

A Love Driven Man lets God transform the pain from the past to open up his heart towards the future.

How to transform pain #1: Making discomfort enjoyable

How to transform pain #2: Using envy as a hint

Reflection Questions:

What happened in your life that caused you a great deal of pain?

Are you offering up your pain to God, or are you running from it?

Is Jesus your healer, or did you mind declare that the pain is "incurable"?

How are you making the discomfort of growth enjoyable?

What makes you envious? What is the envy telling you?

Chapter 5: Taking Steps of Faith

Does my mind have the final say,
or do I give God space to work miracles?

"Trust in the Lord with all your heart, and do not rely on your own insight. In all your ways acknowledge him, and he will make straight your paths."
Proverbs 3:5-6 (NRSV)

A Control Driven Man makes decisions based on what he sees, which results in giving his mind the final say.

A Love Driven Man takes steps of faith to see more of God's Hand in his life.

How to take steps of faith #1: Giving time without expectations

How to take steps of faith #2: Relying on God for results

Reflection Questions:

What life problems seem insolvable to your mind?

Are they genuinely unsolvable, or is your mind just stuck in the past?

Is your mind clinging to God or the past hurts?

How can you give more time without expectations?

How can you rely more on God for results?

Chapter 6: Keeping God #1
Am I trying to become a god, or is God #1 in my life?

"What profit is the idol when its maker has carved it, Or an image, a teacher of falsehood? For its maker trusts in his own handiwork when he fashions speechless idols."
Habakkuk 2:18 (NASB)

A Control Driven Man idolizes capabilities, which results in him trying to become a god.

A Love Driven Man focuses on allowing God to lead in his life to make sure that God is # 1.

How to allow God to lead #1: Preventing tactics from running your strategy

How to allow God to lead #2: Restarting with God

Reflection Questions:

Are you seeking satisfaction in something other than God?

Is God #1 in your life, or are the current trends of today dictating your life?

Are you giving God control, or are you trying to become your own god?

How do you make sure that tactics are not running your strategy?

When you experience setbacks, what helps you restart with God?

Chapter 7: Taking Action
Am I telling myself it's too late, or am I taking action?

"For I know the plans I have for you,' declares the LORD, 'plans to prosper you and not to harm you, plans to give you hope and a future."
Jeremiah 29:11 (NIV)

A Control Driven Man leads his life in a rigid sequence, which results in assuming that *"it's too late for changes."*

A Love Driven Man leads by example to inspire others to action.

How to lead with action #1: Bringing a brick, not a cathedral

How to lead with action #2: Doing the death bed test

Reflection Questions:

When do you tell yourself it's too late?

What prevents you from taking a step of faith?

Are you listening to God or your past?

What helps you bring a brick, not a cathedral?

How often do you do the death bed test?

Chapter 8: Progress Measurement

Am I focusing on the right type of progress?

"We also rejoice in our sufferings, because we know that suffering produces perseverance; perseverance, character; and character, hope. And hope does not disappoint us."
Romans 5:3-5 (BSB)

A Control Driven Man looks for physical progress, which brings temporary happiness.

A Love Driven Man looks for emotional growth that brings sustainable joy.

How do you know this Love Driven thing is working? #1: Laughing at setbacks

How do you know this Love Driven thing is working? #2: Finding a deeper purpose behind the slow progress

Reflection Questions:

How do you measure your life's progress?

Does your way of measuring life's progress bring you joy?

How do you know your heart is opening up to what matters eternally?

How often do you laugh at your setbacks?

What helps you find a deeper purpose behind slow progress?

About the Author

Marek Rudak was born and grew up in communist Poland. He lost his dad at a young age. When he was fourteen, his mom remarried, and Marek moved to California.

He came to feel like he was the fifth wheel in his new family. This led him toward a desire to control others by focusing on earning his worth through personal accomplishments.

Marek graduated in the top 10% of his class at West Point and became a Ranger in the 82nd Airborne Division, where he deployed to Iraq and Afghanistan. After receiving an honorable discharge from the Army, Marek went with the highest paying job he could find, ExxonMobil, where he worked for ten years on multi-billion-dollar projects all over the world.

A tough divorce led Marek to a lot of soul searching and multiple life changes. After meeting the love of his life, Marek decided to quit his job and commit himself full time to the mission of improving men's love proficiency.

For more information, please be sure to visit www.cs1mindset.com.

End Notes

1 Bowen, Will "Complaint Free Relationships: Transforming Your Life One Relationship At A Time" Pub: Virgin Books, 1st Ed 2007.
2 "Siberian Boy, 7, raised by dogs after parents abandoned him." The Independent, August 4, 2004 https://www.independent.co.uk/news/world/europe/siberian-boy-7-raised-by-dogs-after-parents-abandoned-him-555343.html
3 https://www.youtube.com/watch?v=28Ars24c38w
4 Letter to Representative Joseph W. Martin, Jr., (20 March 1951); read to the House by Martin on April 5.
5 The Matrix Reloaded, 2003, Warner Bros, Keanu Reeves and Collin Chou
6 "Metric/Imperial Conversion Errors – The Mars Climate Orbiter: A Million Dollar Mistake" – LibreTexts.org Chemistry – August 15, 2019 - https://chem.libretexts.org/Bookshelves/Analytical_Chemistry/Supplemental_Modules_(Analytical_Chemistry)/Quantifying_Nature/Units_of_Measure/Metric%2F%2FImperial_Conversion_Errors
7 https://www.greatbigstory.com/stories/rock-balancing-that-s-amazing
8 Live2Lead-The Woodlands 2018, Friday, November 2, 2018 at 8 AM – 2:30 PM, The Woodlands United Methodist Church, 2200 Lake Woodlands Dr, The Woodlands, TX 77380
9 Words of Wisdom: "Never Despise Small Beginnings"-Tyler Perry – by Brittany Shawnte September 11, 2019 -https://imperfectlyb.com/2019/09/11/words-of-wisdom-never-despise-small-beginnings-tyler-perry/
10 "Frankenstein" by Mary Shelley. Chapter 20 page 3
11 Oxford, Lexico Dictionary - https://www.lexico.com/definition/new_age
12 "Breaking Down Energy: What You Need To Know as a Coach, Leader, Educator (or Human Being) – Luke Iorio, IPEC Coaching https://www.ipeccoaching.com/blog/breaking-down-energy
13 Sinek, Simon, "Start with Why," Book Corner Publications (2019)
14 Brainy Quote - Pierre Teilhard de Chardin https://www.brainyquote.com/quotes/pierre_teilhard_de_chardi_160888
15 Pusey, Edward Bouverie. (1909-1914) "The Confessions of Saint Augustine Book VIII" – Sacred-Texts.com
16 Midwest Augustinians – "Conversion of Saint Augustine" - https://www.midwestaugustinians.org/conversion-of-st-augustine
17 Leo Tolstoy, "The Death Of Ivan Iilych" – Amazon Kindle Edition
18 Ware, Bonnie, The Top Five Regrets of the Dying: A Life Transformed by the Dearly Departing – Hay House, Inc, 2012 - https://bronnieware.com/blog/regrets-of-the-dying/
19 Roger von Oech, A Whack on the Side of the Head, Mjf Books 2002
20 "Resilience" by Dr. Tony Alessandra http://www.alessandra.com/resilience.html
21 https://www.youtube.com/user/GaryVaynerchuk
22 Live2Lead-The Woodlands, Friday, October 25, 2019 at 8 AM – 2:30 PM, The Pavilion Event Center 2005 Lake Robbins Drive, The Woodlands, TX 77380
23 https://www.youtube.com/watch?v=JA7G7AV-LT8
24 Bill Gates – Quotes – Quotable Quotes – Goodreads.com https://www.goodreads.com/quotes/302999-most-people-overestimate-what-they-can-do-in-one-year

www.ingramcontent.com/pod-product-compliance
Lightning Source LLC
Chambersburg PA
CBHW032127090426
42743CB00007B/492